Lecture Notes in Computer Scie

T0237782

Commenced Publication in 1973
Founding and Former Series Editors:
Gerhard Goos, Juris Hartmanis, and Jan van Leeuwen

Ian Oakley   Stephen Brewster (Eds.)

Haptic and Audio Interaction Design

Second International Workshop, HAID 2007
Seoul, South Korea, November 29-30, 2007
Proceedings

 Springer

Volume Editors

Ian Oakley
Electronics and Telecommunications Research Institute
Smart Interface Research Team
161 Gaejeong-dong, Yuseong-gu, Daejeon 305-700, South Korea
E-mail: ian@etri.re.kr

Stephen Brewster
University of Glasgow
Department of Computing Science
Glasgow G12 8QQ, UK
E-mail: stephen@dcs.gla.ac.uk

Library of Congress Control Number: 2007938601

CR Subject Classification (1998): H.5.2, H.5, H.3, H.4, K.4, K.3

LNCS Sublibrary: SL 3 – Information Systems and Application, incl. Internet/Web and HCI

ISSN   0302-9743
ISBN-10   3-540-76701-0 Springer Berlin Heidelberg New York
ISBN-13   978-3-540-76701-5 Springer Berlin Heidelberg New York

Springer is a part of Springer Science+Business Media

springer.com

© Springer-Verlag Berlin Heidelberg 2007
Printed in Germany

Typesetting: Camera-ready by author, data conversion by Scientific Publishing Services, Chennai, India
Printed on acid-free paper   SPIN: 12189427   06/3180   5 4 3 2 1 0

Preface

Overview

The 2nd International Workshop on Haptic and Audio Interaction Design was held in November 2007 in Seoul, Korea and followed a successful first workshop in Glasgow, UK in 2006. The 2007 event was sponsored by the Korean Ministry of Information and Communication, the Korean Institute of Next-Generation Computing, and the Association of Next-Generation Computing Industry. We remain grateful to these institutions and the generous support they extended towards us. The main focus of the HAID workshop series is to draw together researchers around the theme of human – computer interaction using the modalities of sound and touch. It addresses questions such as how to combine sound and touch interaction together most effectively. Or, are there situations in which one modality offers benefits over the other? Are there situations in which sound and touch offer unique benefits, or alternatively, in which they are inappropriate? Which design formalisms and frameworks can specifically benefit researchers considering multimodal interfaces?

A total of 12 papers were accepted to HAID 2007, each containing novel work on these human-centric topics. Each paper was reviewed by a panel of experts composed of leading figures from both industry and academia. We extend our thanks to all our reviewers, without whom the workshop could not take place. Their diligent efforts and constructive criticisms enriched the quality of the papers considerably. Two invited submissions from our keynote speakers are also included in the proceedings. We were pleased to receive a full paper from James A. Ballas of the US Naval Research Laboratory and an extended abstract from Dong-Soo Kwon, who directs the Human – Robot Interaction Research Centre at the Korea Advanced Institute of Science and Technology. Dr Ballas presented an informative discussion about the links between the most intimate of sensory cues: the sounds and feelings produced by our own bodies. Professor Kwon provided an overview of the history of haptics research and speculated about its future, in particular highlighting how touch might be deployed in mobile devices.

The main track of papers covered considerable thematic ground, from design guidelines to technical implementations; this is an area which is developing on many fronts simultaneously. However, one trend which stands out is the focus on interaction with computational systems, but not computers. Mobile interaction and wearable displays feature prominently, as do tasks such as communication and real-world navigation. This suggests that the future of haptic and audio interactions may well be away from the desktop and out and about on streets and in homes. As computers disappear into the fabric of our living environments, it may well be that we increasingly rely on our senses of hearing and touch to command, control, and understand them. Indeed, there is a sense of inevitability to this. In a pervasive vision of the future, surrounded by a plethora of unseen devices, we must surely rely on our other senses for interaction.

We provide an overview of the topics and foci of the papers below.

Tactile Displays

Research on tactile displays has been developing rapidly, in part because of their wide deployment in mobile phones and other handheld devices. In many cases, the underlying technology is simple and cheap and there is a general feeling that it could be put to many more constructive uses than simply indicating the arrival of a call. One key way to achieve this is through using multiple tactile actuators, an approach adopted by all the authors in this session. Lee et al. describe a wearable system which displays tactile cues directly derived from the environment to a user's fingertip, allowing them to feel at a distance. Hoggan et al. discuss a system based on mounting multiple tactile actuators to the exterior of a PDA and relate several experiments determining whether its users can effectively discriminate from which ones stimuli originate. Finally, Kyung et al. describe a new design for a miniature tactile display which can stimulate the fingertip and several studies of its effectiveness in fundamental tasks such as texture and shape perception.

Communication and Games

Haptics and audio are indivisibly linked with communication and entertainment, and this session explores new ways to express this synergy. Seeking to add expressivity and richness to mobile communications, Brown and Williamson describe the design of a novel method of sending short messages based on gestural input and tactile and audio output. At the other end of the project lifecycle, Baurley et al. discuss the situated qualitative evaluation of a wearable computing system which can convey interpersonal gestures such as hugs and strokes to the forearm. Kim and Kim describe a racing game, intended for use on mobile phones, which incorporates tactile cues to overcome the fundamental restrictions of small screen sizes. Can haptics and audio cues effectively convey emotions and create immersion and presence? The papers in this session address this demanding question.

Accessibility and Navigation

Access technologies intended to support visually impaired users remain a key domain for haptic and audio interaction design: these users rely on non-visual feedback for everything they do. Consequently, they require efficient and effective interactive systems. Two papers in this session contribute to this body of research. Shin and Lim describe a wearable computing system which integrates range-finding sensors, body tracking and vibrotactile and audio displays to enable visually impaired users to navigate safely in their immediate environment, avoiding potential obstacles. Pielot et al. support the other stage of this process: route planning, rather than on-the-spot navigation. They describe a tangible interface which allows visually impaired users to explore an audio map, learning the locations of key landmarks by referencing the sounds they make. Kim and Kwon discuss a slightly different topic, namely, how haptic and audio cues can aid users in the complex task of accurately navigating around a three-dimensional virtual environment which is displayed on a flat, two-dimensional screen. As three-dimensional interfaces become more commonplace, this is a problem which will only become more widespread, and Kim and Kwon's work suggests multimodal interaction may be one way to address it.

Design

As human – computer interaction matures as a discipline, the role of design is becoming more and more important. As it lacks a basis in widely applicable theories which yield consistent and predictable results, more informal structures have come to the fore: methodologies, guidelines, and principles. The papers in this session contribute to this practical, hands-on body of work. Bjelland and Tangeland discuss how the use of early-stage haptic prototypes might benefit a user-centered design process and present a case study of this in action. They conclude with recommendations for best practices to adopt while prototyping haptic interfaces. Oakley and Park discuss how to best design for eyes-free interaction, referring to systems which enable simple, rapid, and confident input without occupying visual attention. They review the literature, present a set of design principles, and describe a case study embodying these. Finally, Pirhonen et al. present a design methodology for creating rich, detailed, and effective audio interfaces. Based on detailed use scenarios and personas, the technique espouses iterative presentation of audio interfaces to panels of designers to generate consistent and refined feedback schemes. As with the other papers in this session, they conclude with a detailed case study illustrating their technique.

User interfaces remain predominantly visual, but these papers show there are many specific scenarios, and indeed much to gain, by incorporating haptic and audio elements. Our environment is composed of not only sights, but also a vibrant range of sounds, touches, smells, and tastes. HAID 2007 presented research motivated to making our interactions with computational systems equally rich.

November 2007

Ian Oakley
Stephen Brewster

Organization

The 2nd International Workshop on Haptic and Audio Interaction Design was organized by the Electronics and Telecommunications Research Institute (ETRI), Daejeon, Korea and the University of Glasgow, UK.

Workshop Chair

Dong-Won Han (ETRI, Korea)

Organization Chair

Cheol-Su Lim (Seokyeong University, Korea)

Organizing Committee

Byeong-Seok Shin (Inha University, Korea)
Yong-Soon Kim (The Association of Next-Generation Computing Industry, Korea)

Progam Chairs

Papers   Ian Oakley (ETRI, Korea)
                          Stephen Brewster (University of Glasgow, UK)
Posters and Demos   Lorna Brown (Microsoft Research, UK)
                          Tae-Jeong Jang (Kangwon National University, Korea)

Program Committee

Nick Avis, University of Cardiff, UK
Federico Barbagli, Stanford Robotics Lab and Hansen Medical, USA
Stephen Barrass, University of Canberra, Australia
Seungmoon Choi, Pohang University of Science and Engineering, Korea
Abdulmotaleb El Saddik, University of Ottawa, Canada
Mikael Fernstrom, University of Limerick, Ireland
Antonio Frisoli, Scuola Superiore Sant'Anna, Italy
Stephen Furner, British Telecom, UK
Matti Grohn, CSC Scientific Computing, Finland
Matthias Harders, ETH Zurich, Switzerland
Steven Hsiao, Johns Hopkins University, USA

Sponsoring Institutions

 MINISTRY OF INFORMATION AND COMMUNICATION REPUBLIC OF KOREA

 Korean Institute of Next Generation Computing

 Association of Next Generation Computing Industry

ETRI
www.etri.re.kr

UNIVERSITY
of
GLASGOW

Table of Contents

Plenary Talks

Session: Tactile Displays

Session: Communication and Games

Session: Accessibility and Navigation

Session: Design

Self-produced Sound: Tightly Binding Haptics and Audio

James A. Ballas

Naval Research Laboratory
Washington, DC, USA
james.ballas@nrl.navy.mil

Abstract. This paper discusses the concept of self-produced sound and its importance in understanding audio-haptic interaction. Self-produced sound is an important stimulus in understanding audio-haptic interaction because of the tight binding between the two modalities. This paper provides background on this type of sound, a brief review of the asynchrony and neurophysiology research that has addressed the cross-modality interaction, and examples of research into self-produced sound, including a unique but common instance: sound produced when consuming food.

Keywords: Haptics, self-produced sound, hearing, psychoacoustics.

1 Introduction

No formal definition of self-produced sound exists. Here, it is sound that is produced by one's own body or body movements[1]. The sound waves are produced by movement of the limbs or mouth interacting with the body itself or with external surfaces or objects. Examples of interactions between body components include teeth grinding, finger snapping, and coughing. Examples of interactions between the body components and external surfaces include footsteps, clothing sound, and chewing of foods. These sounds are transmitted to the ear not only through air conduction, but in the case of many sounds, also through bone conduction. For example, the hearing of chewing sounds will be transmitted primarily via bone conduction.

At the onset, it is fair to ask whether this type of sound involves haptics in any reasonable sense of that term. Using the Gibsonian definition [2] of the haptic system as "the perceptual system by which animals and men are *literally* in touch with the environment," self-produced sound is produced whenever the touching behavior is the physical cause of the auditory event. Because the actuator of the sound is the haptic system, and the sensing of both haptics and sound are self-contained with the actuation mechanism, there is a tight binding between haptics and sound in both actuation and reception.

This forms the basis of the special character of self-produced sound in understanding the interaction of haptics and audio. The binding between the haptic

---

[1] Obviously the sound of one's own voice is a self-produced sound, but is not included in this paper because it doen not involve haptics in the common sense of that term. See Truax [1] for an excellent description of the voice as a self-produced sound.

I. Oakley and S. Brewster (Eds.): HAID 2007, LNCS 4813, pp. 1–8, 2007.

system movement and the sound is tightly coupled such that it seems unlikely that this coupling can be dissociated through task instructions. That is, the associative linkage between the haptic and sound for self-produced sound might be an obligatory outcome of sensory-perceptual processing. The test for obligatory processing typically involves neuroimaging techniques. Studies have demonstrated that obligatory processing is present when neuroimaging shows processing of a particular type or form has occurred even when the subject's task does not require it (see [3] for an example of an obligatory processing study). To my knowledge, no such studies of haptic-audio interaction have been done; this would be a topic for future research.

Some insight into the special character of self-produced sound can be obtained by examining studies that have examined haptic-audio asynchrony. It is reasonable to hypothesize that these studies should show lower asynchrony thresholds for self-produced sound because this type of sound embodies neural activity of both haptic and sonic events. In effect, the judgmental bias that can be present in a temporal decision, i.e., the Greenwich Observatory phenomenon documented by Maskelyne, is less likely to occur for self-produced sound. Three studies are briefly reviewed that address this topic.

Levitin et al. [4] utilized two observers in an asynchrony experiment that involved a type of drumming that was heard and either felt or seen. They compared the asynchrony estimates made by an observer who saw the action and heard the impact sound to those of an actor who performed the action thus feeling the event and also heard the sound. The asynchrony of the impact and the sound was manipulated. Their results clearly showed that the actor who produced, felt and heard the impact made more accurate simultaneity judgments than the observer. However, this study involved a comparison between haptic-audio and visual-audio asynchrony, and does not explicitly address the tight coupling between haptics and audio that occurs with self-produced sound.

Two other asynchrony studies separately used self-produced and externally generated sound. Adelstein et al. [5] developed a system that produced the type of self-produced sound that occurs when you use a hammer to strike an object. They attached an accelerometer to a hammer and conditioned the signal that was produced when the hammer hit a surface so as to produce a TTL pulse upon impact. This pulse was then used to generate an audio pulse, with variable delays introduced. The base processing latency of the system was ~7 ms, so the experimental design was limited to only producing audio-lagging of ~7 ms or more. In contrast to other asynchrony studies, they did not include any stimuli with the audio leading the haptic event. Their analysis included calculation of Point of Subjective Equality (PSE) and Just Noticeable Differences (JNDs). They found JNDs that were much smaller than Levitin found, and with the best subject, saw asynchrony judgments that approach the limits of auditory fusion (1-2 ms). It bears noting that they intentionally masked the actual self-produced sound of the hammer hitting the target object.

Externally generated sound sources were used in an asynchrony study by Martens and Woszczyk [6]. Their system produced whole body vertical movement for the haptic event and an indirect audio signal from an array of 5 low-frequency drivers and 32 high frequency drivers. The sound signal was an impact recorded from dropping a stack of telephone books on the floor. They used a staircase tracking paradigm with a 2-alternative forced choice between whether the audio was earlier or later than the haptic movement. The asynchrony was varied between +/- 40 ms with a minimum asynchrony of 10 ms. They found that simultaneity accuracy (both presented simultaneously) was .7 and .8 for the two subjects. Haptic leading asynchrony was almost never judged to be simultaneous. Haptic lagging asynchrony was misjudged to be simultaneous about 20-40% when the asynchronies were 10-20 ms. There was little difference in accuracy between 20-30 ms asynchronies. Although their data cannot be compared directly with Adelstein, the lack of a difference between 10-20 ms suggests that the JNDs for their task were greater than those found by Adelstein.

At this time, the limited research on asynchrony judgments cannot provide any definite answer as to whether the tight binding between haptics and audio with self-produced sound will support more accurate synchrony judgments. But the work to date is consistent with the hypothesis that this type of sound involves tightly coupled haptic-audio interaction. The basis of this binding would lie in the neurophysiology of haptic-audio convergence, which is briefly described in the next section.

2 Neurophysiology of Audio-Haptic Interaction

The traditional view of multisensory convergence is that unisensory processing must be essentially complete before multisensory processing can occur. This view assumes that multisensory convergence occurs at the higher cortical areas thought to be used for integration functions. However, this traditional view has been challenged by recent work that has shown that convergence occurs not only early in cortical processing but also subcortically (Fig. 1).

2.1 Subcortical Convergence

An example of subcortical convergence is the work by Kanold and Young [7], who studied the interaction between the auditory and somatosensory systems in the cat, which has a moveable pinna that can be oriented for active auditory exploration. They found that the dorsal cochlear nucleus (DCN), which is one level above the cochlea, receives information from the medullary somatosensory nuclei (MSN) that are associated with pinna muscle movement. They found that stimulation of the cervical nerves associated with pinna muscle movement produced activation in the DCN. They speculated that this subcortical convergence is used to correct for changes in the auditory spectrum produced by pinna movement. The analogous process in the human system would be a subcortical interaction that would connect a neural coding of head azimuth position to the auditory system so that spectral changes due to the head-related transfer function could be used to correct the spectrum of a heard sound.

2.2 Cortical Convergence

Several studies have shown that cortical convergence is found in early sensory processing areas of the auditory cortex [8,9]. Fu et al. [8] investigated somatosensory inputs to the caudomedial (CM) auditory cortex, which is a second stage cortical structure. They found that cutaneous stimulation of head, neck and hand areas produced CM activation, concurrently with activation from auditory stimuli. They

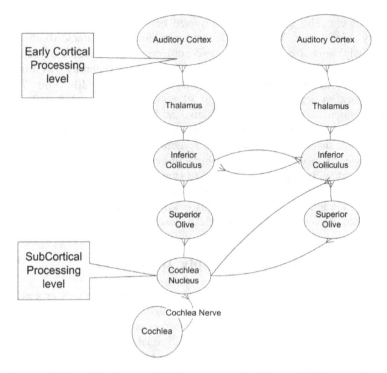

Fig. 1. A general view of the layers of auditory processing illustrating where auditory-haptic convergence has been found at both subcortical and early cortical levels

also observed some CM responses to proprioceptive and vibration stimulation. Kayser et al. [9] investigated somatosensory and auditory interaction using functional magnetic resonance imaging (fMRI). With broad-band noise as an auditory stimulus, and cutaneous stimulation of hand and foot areas as a tactical stimulus, they found that activity in the caudal auditory belt (CAB) demonstrated two fundamental principles of multisensory interaction: temporal coincidence and inverse effectiveness. Temporal coincidence means that stimulation from different modalities that is temporally coincident should exhibit more integration than stimulation that is not coincident. They compared the effects of auditory and cutaneous pulses that were either coincident or out of phase, and found greater integration with coincident stimuli in CAB areas. The principal of inverse effectiveness means that cross modal integration should be more effective, in a relative sense, when the stimulus is weak in one of the modalities. Through variation in the intensity of the sound, they found that cross modality integration was greater when the sound was quieter. In addition, their tactal stimulus had relatively minor effects in the auditory areas on its own, but enhanced the auditory stimulus when presented in combination. While temporal coincidence and inverse effectivness can occur with either self-produced or externally generated sound, both phenomena might be more prevalant when there is the coincident presence of a motor movement, a felt haptic sensation, and near-field sound that is sensed through air conduction and perhaps through bone conduction.

3 Self-produced Sound Studies

Research on self-produced sound is limited and scattered across different disciplines. This section describes a few works that have investigated this type of sound.

3.1 Taxonomy

The World Soundscape Project included the collection and documentation of references to sound in literature, and catalogued these into what is a general taxonomy of sound [10]. The taxonomy included a category for human sounds. Its constituents included the following types of sounds: Voice, Body, Clothing, and Humans in Groups. Two of these categories are of interest here, Body sounds and Clothing sounds. The literature references found for each of these types included the types of sounds listed under each category in the Table 1.

Table 1. Instances of two types of self-produced sound found in general literature. This work was part of the World Soundscape Project. Details are available at http://www.sfu.ca/sonic-studio/srs/.

Sounds of the Body	Sounds of Clothing
Heartbeat, Breathing, Footsteps, Hands (Clapping, etc.), Stomach, Eating, Drinking , Evacuating, Lovemaking, Nervous System, Sleeping, Decomposition, Dying, Belches, Flatulence, Smoking, Fighting, Sneezing, Pain	Clothing, Pipe, Jewelery, Bags, Satchels, etc., Hand-fan, Shoes

Most of the instances are self explanatory except for the sound of the nervous system and the sound of pain. The literature references in these two cases are metaphorical descriptions of sound. The sound of pain is from D. H. Lawrence's *England, My England* (Penguin, 1966, p. 38)

"There was a resounding of pain. It seemed to resound from the outside of his consciousness: like a loud bell clanging very near. Yet he knew it was himself. He must associate himself with it. After a lapse and a new effort, he identified a pain in his head, a large pain that clanged and resounded."

The sound of the nervous system is this phrase from Remarque's *All Quiet on the Western Front* (Little, Brown & Co., Boston, 1929, p. 70): "Inside the gas-mask my head booms and roars…"

3.2 Incidence or Occurrence

As part of a general investigation into the types of factors that are involved in identification of everyday sounds, Ballas [11] conducted a survey intended to document the occurrence frequency of distinctly different sounds (different in that they are generated by different types of events). Students were asked to document the sounds that they heard in their daily life. A pseudo random, time-based sampling technique was used. Each student was provided with a timer and a set of time periods to enter into the timer. Upon setting the timer, the student continued their normal activity. When the timer went off, the student recorded the last sound that they had heard, or a concurrent sound if one was present when the timer went off. They were asked not to include speech sounds, but were not given any special instructions about self-produced sound. Instances of self-produced sound were reported. These are listed in Table 2 with the occurrence frequency for each instance.

Table 2. Occurrence frequency of self-produced sound from Ballas [11]

Sound	Occurrence Frequency
Footsteps	70
Chewing	13
Cough	6
Clearing throat	6
Clothes rustling	6
Snapping gum	3
Drinking	3
Hiccups	2
Scratching clothes	2

The occurrence frequencies can be converted into a probability of hearing the sound. Taking the total of all the sounds listed in Table 2, the probability of hearing a self-produced sound was estimated to be .09 within a selected sample interval during awake hours. While this is low for any single sample interval, the cumulative probability across sample intervals (assuming that samples are independent) will quickly rise to a value that makes it highly likely you will have heard such a sound. One caveat that should be mentioned is that the students did not record who generated the sound, and it is likely that, for example, many of the footsteps heard were made by other individuals. This illustrates another aspect of self-produced sound; it is definitive evidence that a person is present.

3.3 Food Studies

The food industry has an interest in understanding the process of food consumption including both the somatosensory and auditory sensations that are perceived when chewing and swallowing food products. A considerable body of research is conducted, much of it published in the Journal of Texture Studies. Some of the research addresses the acoustic properties of biting, chewing and other mouth sounds. Some general findings about the acoustics of eating crispy foods are worth mentioning [12]. The duration of the sound of eating events ranges from a few hundred ms to 203 s. Biting a crisp biscuit takes about 200 ms. The sound pulse of this type of biting has a pressure change of about 100dB. The effective sound level is about 60-70 dB.

Many of the studies include sensory, instrumental and acoustic analyses of food and its consumption. Sensory analysis typically includes subjective assessments of the food and its consumption on scales such as crispness, juiciness, fibrousness, etc. The subjects are often trained evaluators. Instrumental analyses include measurements of the food using compression testing, ultrasonic wave propagation, fracturing, etc. Acoustic analyses include recording of bite sounds or food compression sounds and subsequent spectral processing of the recording. Many of the research studies include information about the haptics of the mouth when chewing and the related auditory sounds. The analysis of this information seeks to understand relationships between these haptic and auditory data, and how they individually or jointly relate to subjective sensory judgments.

Some of these multivariate research studies focus on understanding phenomena related to crunchy and crisp foods, such as breakfast cereal and apples. For example, Barreiro et al. [13] investigated the factors associated with judging apples to be mealy. For background, it is useful to understand that when a crisp vegetable is fractured, the cell walls break releasing juice and providing a sensation of crispiness through both haptic and auditory sensations. Mealy apples have more air in the cells, instead of juice, and the cell walls are less likely to break with fracture. The objective of their study was to determine what physical factors were associated with key sensory judgments, and develop a methodology to quantify these factors.

The apple samples consisted of three varieties, harvested at different times of fruit maturity. Subjects rated the samples on texture (both at first bite and in subsequent chewing), on flavor (when chewing and after swallowing), and on internal appearance and odor (the apples were peeled). Acoustic impulse response measurements were made when the apple was struck with a rod. This impulse response was used to compute a measure of stiffness. Compression and decompression of the samples were performed to compute the hardness and juice content, and wave propagation was calculated to determine the sound speed inside the apple. The results showed significant relationships (correlations $> .80$) between sensory judgments and instrumental measurements. Their work touched on haptic perception through the assessment of crispness when chewing. A regression analysis found that crispness was significantly related ($R^2 = .71$) to three instrumental parameters: absorbed energy, restitution energy (both computed from the compression test), and stiffness computed from the acoustic impulse response. Interestingly, it might be possible to determine the mealiness of an apple by using the same test suggested for larger fruits—listening to the sound when you tap it.

4　Conclusion

The objective of this paper was to introduce and describe a type of sound that has received little focused attention despite its apparent importance in understanding haptic-audio interaction. One of the reasons self-produced sound has received little work is the inherent challenge in doing research on this topic. For example, it is impossible to vary the temporal asynchrony between the actual sensations of feeling and hearing an impact when you touch a surface. However, much of the research here illustrates that work on this topic is possible, but it takes ingenuity and sometimes sophisticated technology. In fact, much of the research on the topic is recent only because new technology has been utilized in innovative ways. It is expected that more research on this topic will be forthcoming.

Acknowledgments. The preparation of this paper was sponsored by the U. S. Naval Research Laboratory and the Office of Naval Research. The views and conclusions expressed in this paper are those of the author and do not reflect the official policies, either expressed or implied of the U. S. Navy. The author appreciates the comments from Justin Nevitt and Judith Ladd on early versions of the manuscript.

References

1. Truax, B.: Acoustic Communication. Ablex, Norwood, NJ (1984)
2. Gibson, J.J.: The Senses Considered as Perceptual Systems. Houghton Mifflin, Boston (1966)
3. Orgs, G., Lange, K., Dombrowski, J., Heil, M.: Is conceptual priming for environmental sounds obligatory? International Journal of Psychophysiology 65, 162–166 (2007)
4. Levitin, D.J., MacLean, K., Mathews, M., Chu, L., Jensen, E.: The perception of cross-modal simultaneity (Or "The Greenwich Observatory Problem" Revisited). In: Computing Anticipatory Systems: CASYS 1999 - Third International Conference, pp. 323–329 (2000)
5. Adelstein, B.D., Begault, D.R., Anderson, M.R., Wenzel, E.M.: Sensitivity to Haptic-Audio Asynchrony. In: 5th International Conference on Multimodal Interfaces, Vancouver, Canada, pp. 73–76. ACM Press, New York (2003)
6. Martens, W.L., Woszczyk, W.: Perceived Synchrony in a Bimodal Display: Optimal Intermodal Delay for Coordinated Auditory and Haptic Reproduction. In: Proceedings of ICAD 04-Tenth Meeting of the International Conference on Auditory Display, Sydney, Australia (2004)
7. Kanold, P.O., Young, E.O.: Proprioceptive Information from the Pinna Provides Somatosensory Input to Cat Dorsal Cochlear Nucleus. The Journal of Neuroscience 21, 7848–7858 (2001)
8. Fu, K.G., Johnston, T.A., Shah, A.S., Arnold, L., Smiley, J., Hackett, T.A., Garraghty, P.E., Schroeder, C.E.: Auditory Cortical Neurons Respond to Somatosensory Stimulation. J. Neuroscience 23, 7510–7515 (2003)
9. Kayser, C., Petkov, C.I., Augath, M., Logothetis, N.K.: Integration of Touch and Sound in Auditory Cortex. Neuron 48, 373–384 (2005)
10. Schafer, R.M.: Our Sonic Environment and the Soundscape: The Tuning of the World. Destiny Books, Rochester, Vermont (1994)
11. Ballas, J.A.: Common Factors in the identification of an assortment of brief everyday sounds. Journal of Experimental Psychology: Human Perception and Performance 19, 250–267 (1993)
12. Luyten, H., Vliet, T.V.: Acoustic Emission, Fracture Behavior and Morphology of Dry Crispy Foods: A Discussion Article. Journal of Texture Studies 37, 221–240 (2006)
13. Barreiro, P., Ortiz, C., Ruiz-Altisent, M., De Smedt, V., Schotte, S., Andani, Z., Wakeling, I., Beyts, P.K.: Comparison between Sensory and Instrumental Measurements for Mealiness Assessment in Apples. A Collaborative Test. Journal of Texture Studies 29, 509–525 (1998)

Will Haptics Technology Be Used in Mobile Devices?: A Historical Review of Haptics Technology and Its Potential Applications in Multi-modal Interfaces

Dong-Soo Kwon

Human Robot Interaction Research Center, KAIST
335 Gwahangno, Yuseong-gu, Daejon 305-701, Republic of Korea
kwonds@kaist.ac.kr
http://robot.kaist.ac.kr

1 Extended Abstract

In recent years, the haptics research area has become an interdisciplinary field covering perception, psychophysics, neuroscience, mechanism design, control, virtual reality, and human computer interaction. If we try to identify the origins of haptics research, it can be said to have emerged from the teleoperator systems of the late 1940s. In these initial explorations, increasing the transparency level of the mechanical master/slave manipulator system was the main issue as such imrpovements promised higher levels of task efficiency. For example, in order to handle nuclear materials effectively inside a radiation shielded room, minimizing friction and the effects of inertia in a mechanical master/slave system was the critical factor. Furthermore, when teleoperator systems were designed for hazardous environments and long distance space applications, establishing stability in the face of lengthy (and often uncertain) time delays was the key issue. Ergonomic design of the remote control console and the master haptic device also exerted a strong influence on how effectively remote information could be displayed to enhance telepresence.

As computer graphics technology has advanced sufficiently to realize a wide range of virtual reality applications, the development of control technologies and haptic master device designs has adapted to be predominantly focused on interaction with virtual environments. There have been numerous breakthroughs in visual, sound, and haptic modeling technologies which together now enable the real-time display of contact with virtual objects including things such as shape deformation and reactive force. There have also been attempts to model and display the fine details of touched surfaces in order to enhance virtual presence. Studies in neuroscience and psychophysics have revealed the human perceptual processes underlying haptic sensations. Drawing on this understanding, research has also begun to examine how to best construct tactile display units capable of rendering feelings of roughness, softness and temperature.

Recently, the communication industry has commercialized phones which enable high quality video conferencing in a mobile form factor. Given these advances, they are currently looking for technologies that provide haptic sensations as these may form a more intuitive user interface. However, the limitations of the mobile form factor are stringent; any haptic display unit must be small and consume little power.

I. Oakley and S. Brewster (Eds.): HAID 2007, LNCS 4813, pp. 9–10, 2007.
© Springer-Verlag Berlin Heidelberg 2007

In this keynote talk, I will present a historical review of haptic technology by presenting a spectrum of past and present research. I will address the key issues in the haptics area with the introduction of my laboratory's several related projects. The first haptics research at KAIST was the development of a 6-DOF Force-Feedback Master device intended for teleoperation. Since then our interest has expanded to encompass virtual reality applications for haptics and we developed a grasping mouse system which can display both the shape and the weight of a virtual object by providing force feedback to the fingers and wrist. For more realistic tactile feelings, we also built an integrated tactile display mouse which combines a force feedback mechanism with a pin-array tactile display unit based on piezo-actuators. We also added a thermal display function to this device, completing the development of a holistic haptic display device. This holistic device can render sensations of small-scale shape, texture and temperature by stimulating not only the mechano-receptors but also the thermo-receptors. In an investigation of human touch perception using these devices, we uncovered novel relationships between vibration frequency and perceived roughness.

Recently, the mobile device industry has embraced haptic feedback in the form of simple vibrotactile devices based on eccentric motors. These are now embedded into the majority of PDAs and cellular phones, and many game controllers. But the feedback provided by these devices is crude. This talk will close with a discussion of the requirements of the mobile device industry and our ideas on how to incorporate high fidelity haptic technology into a handheld form factor.

As the future of human-digital device interfaces will support multi-modal interaction including visual, audio, and haptic elements, current developments in haptics technology have huge potential to open up new areas in the communication and display industries as well support further fundamental research into human perception.

Tactile Visualization with Mobile AR
on a Handheld Device

Beom-Chan Lee, Hyeshin Park, Junhun Lee, and Jeha Ryu

Human-Machine-Computer Interface Lab.,
Dept. Mechatronics, Gwangju Institute of Science and Technology, Gwangju, Korea
{bclee,resungod,junhun,ryu}@gist.ac.kr

Abstract. This paper presents a tactile visualization system incorporating touch feedback to a mobile AR system realized on a handheld device. This system enables, for the first time, interactive haptic feedback though mobile and wearable interfaces. To demonstrate the proposed concept, an interactive scenario that helps a visually impaired user to recognize specific pictograms has been constructed. This system allows users to tactually recognize flat pictograms situated in the real world. Furthermore, it also opens the door to a wide range of applications which could be based on wearable tactile interaction.

1 Introduction

The rapid development of mobile computing technology has led to a situation where the widespread availability of increasingly small and inexpensive computers and wireless networking now allows users to roam the real world and remain in contact with distributed, online information sources: they are no longer tethered to stationary machines. Indeed, users are able to access various services through visual and auditory information whenever they want and wherever they are. In addition, combining mobile computing with augmented reality (AR) has been shown to be advantageous in various mobile computing applications as it can provide an intuitive interface to a 3D information space embedded in a real environment [1]. This has been shown in various application areas such as assembly and construction [2,3], maintenance and inspection [4,5], navigation and path finding [6,7,8], tourism [9,10,11], architecture and archaeology [12, 13], urban modeling [14,15,16], entertainment[17,18], and medicine[19]. This body of work makes a compelling case that AR techniques make for efficient and effective mobile computing experiences.

However, existing AR systems in mobile environments have only considered the visual modality and we believe that there exists further potential. Specifically we are concerned with the possibilities afforded by the addition of haptic information to a mobile and wearable AR scenario. Generally, haptic means pertaining to the sense of touch and haptic systems provide users with tactual sensory information about virtual or augmented environments [20]. Haptic systems allow touch exploration and the interactive manipulation of environments through haptic interfaces. Haptic visualization makes it possible to display virtual [21,22,23] or real [24], object geometry [25] to visually impaired or blind persons. However, these haptic visualization systems are

I. Oakley and S. Brewster (Eds.): HAID 2007, LNCS 4813, pp. 11–21, 2007.

typically limited to kinesthetic interaction and consequently are displayed on large mechanical haptic devices. The most crucial drawback for this kind of haptic feedback in mobile environments is the lack of portability of the output devices.

In this paper, therefore, we propose a new tactile visualization method for incorporating the human sense of touch with a mobile AR system. This system enables, for the first time, interactive touch interaction in mobile and wearable environments. To demonstrate and explore this new concept, an interactive scenario that helps a visually impaired person to recognize specific pictograms or signs has been constructed. This system runs on a PDA, a small stand-alone handheld computer. However, since PDAs have limited computing resources, we have devised a software architecture based on optimizing the computing power required for capturing and processing camera images, the generation of tactile information, and transmitting data to the tactile user interface in real-time. To enable touch interaction in a mobile environment, we have devised a wearable tactile user interface based on coin-type vibrating actuators attached to user's finger tip. Previously literature has shown a vibrotactile display can be easily used to display specific information [26,27], letters [28,29,30,31] and the motion or shape of specific objects [26, 32, 33]. This prior work allows us to test the feasibility of using a tactile display for sensory compensation. We also have developed control methodologies which allow us to display more versatile tactile cues on the vibrating actuators. This assists a user in recognizing shapes when touching the captured pictograms.

This paper is organized as follows: Section 2 presents overall system configuration as well as an interactive tactile visualization scenario with mobile and wearable interfaces. The detailed algorithms, system architecture and tactile user interface design which were required to develop the proposed system effectively are described in detail in Section 3. In Section 4, the implementation and demonstration of the proposed tactile visualization system is presented. Finally, conclusions from this work and possible future directions are contained in Section 5.

2   Interactive Tactile Visualization Scenario and Overall System Configuration

The goal of this research is to realize a mobile AR system which incorporates tactile interaction. Specifically, as touch sensations play a particularly important role in the life of visually impaired users, we have constructed an interactive touch scenario which aims to provide a visually impaired person with the ability to 'read' graphical pictogram or symbols. Such signs are commonplace in the form of road signs and information notices, and most users easily recognize and comprehend their meaning. For a visually impaired person, however, it is extremely difficult for them gain awareness of the specific meaning of a sign because the pictograms are generally represented by 2D images. Needless to say, appropriate haptic cues could help them determine the contents of these pictograms. Previously work has shown that tactile maps or diagrams are effective ways to display information to visually impaired users. However a mobile tactile user interface based on vibration motors may not be sufficient to accurately represent a tactile map or diagrams due to the practical limitatations of the motors' arrangement on user's finger. Threfore, it is nessaary to design a novel tactile visualization system for mobile scenarios.

Fig. 1. Conceptual scenario for the tactile visualization

Figure 1 shows a conceptual scenario for the proposed tactile visualization system. It is intended to help visually impaired users in a mobile environment. In this scenario, we assume that the basic locations of pictograms are acquired by another infrastructure (such as RFID technology) and also that the user holds or wears a PDA based system with both a camera and a tactile user interface. In addition, we assume that each pictogram includes a specific marker for determining its exact location. When the user realizes they are in the general area of a pictogram (through an alert delivered by an alternative infrastructure such as RFID), the user can scan their surroundings in detail with the camera. During this process, the precise location of the pictogram is detected by vision based marker traking. When this happens, the system informs the user instantly though auditory and tactile notifications. Now aware of the location of the pictogram, the user is free to explore its shape (as captured by the camera) by touching the PDA's screen with their finger. If a collision is detected between the representation of the pictogram and the user's finger, this is rendered on the tactile display system in the form of vibrations of one or more tactile actuators attached to the user's fingertip.

The proposed tactile visualization with mobile AR on a handheld device is divided into two main parts: a Handheld Mobile Platform (HMP) and a Tactile User Interface (TUI). The handheld mobile platform deals with pictogram detection, processing and tactile data transmission. The tactile user interface system takes charge of tactile control and display corresponding to the user's touch interactions. Figure 2 shows the overall system configuration of the proposed tactile visualization. In order to select a stand-alone mobile platform, we identified three commercially available classes of mobile or wearable computers as potential candidates for handheld AR. These are Tablet PCs, PDAs and cellular phones. All of these possible devices make specific tradeoffs between size, weight, computing resources and cost. Taking into account these factors, we chose the PDA as a target platform. The PDA is a good compromise between weight, size, and processing power.

The role of the HMP can be broken down into detecting pictograms and processing captured images. Pictograms are detected using a standard AR technique which recognizes fiducial markers attached to the pictograms. Once a marker is detected, the captured image is displayed on the PDA screen and processed to determine whether there is a collision between the user's interaction point (with their finger on the screen) and shape of the pictogram. This is achieved by using image processing techniques which have been carefully optimized to the limited computing resources of a PDA.

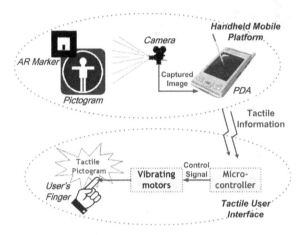

Fig. 2. System configuration

The Tactile User Interface (TUI) consists of micro-controller and tactile actuators. The micro-controller processes the tactile information coming from the PDA over a Bluetooth link. Based on this data it generates control signals to actuate the vibrating motors which are attached to the user's finger. We choose to use a small embedded micro-controller as this provides a highly flexible and cost effective solution to many established embedded control applications. The tactile display itself consists of five actuators intended to be mounted on the fingertip to display contact directions between the fingertip and the contours of the captured pictograms. This process allows users to recognize the pictogram's shape by exploring the touch screen with their fingertip.

3   Software Architecture and Tactile User Interface

In this section, we precisely describe the software architecture used to achieve the vision based pictogram detection and collision processing. In addition, we provide details regarding our tactile user interface and the low-level control algorithm we have developed to enhance recognition of presented pictograms given the limited capacity of vibrating actuators.

3.1   Software Architecture and Pictogram Detection

Since PDAs have limited computing power compared to desktop PCs, it is important to carefully manage computational resources so as to achieve real-time tactile

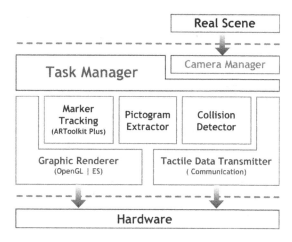

Fig. 3. Software Architecture

visualization in wearable environments. Accordingly, we developed a component based software architecture to accelerate the task of developing applications on a handheld device. This is shown in Figure 3.

At its center lies the Task Manager (TM), a component that supervises the remainder of the system. It plays an important role in stripping away all the functionality deemed unnecessary for running the application on a PDA, where computing resources are scarce. In addition, the TM takes charge of time scheduling so that each sub-component has access to sufficient computational resources.

The Camera Manager (CM) allows the PDA to capture real images and is handled by the TM. The captured images are transferred to the marker tracking module for determining the location of the distributed pictograms. At the same time, the captured image is rendered using the graphic rendering module of the OpenGL|ES API. This is a royalty-free, cross-platform API for full-function 2D and 3D graphics on embedded systems-including consoles, phones, appliances and vehicles [34]. It consists of a well-defined subset of desktop OpenGL, and creates a flexible and powerful low-level interface between software and graphics acceleration. It also enables fully programmable 3D graphics.

The marker tracking module is based on ARToolkit combined with a software library that can be used to calculate camera positions and orientations relative to fiducial markers in real-time [35]. It has been developed to simplify the creation of AR applications. When the captured images are transferred to the marker tracking module, it determines whether they contain the physical markers or not. This marker tracking module enables the location of markers to be detected in real-time.

Once a physical marker is detected, the TM transfers the current image to the Pictogram Extractor (PE), where shape of the pictogram is extracted based on it characteristics in the RGB color space. In general, since the color of pictogram differs greatly from the background color, this analysis is relatively trivial. In addition, user interaction only occurs between the captured image and user's fingertip and so only the region in the image local to the user's finger is processed by pictogram extractor module. The processing region obviously varies according to size of user's fingertip.

By adopting this local image processing technique, the computational demands of the pictogram extractor are minimized without any deterioration in the feel of the interaction.

The Collision Detector (CD) allows users with feel shapes with the tactile interface when the users touch the screen with their fingertip. It detects the exact collision between the point of touch screen input and the pictogram. In the collision detector module, it checks to see if the current input point is inside the current pictogram. Furthermore, the collision depth also can be determined by using the initial collision point and current input point as shown in Figure 4. The penetration depth can be used to determine an actuating intensity for the tactile display system. After the collision detection stage, the results (essentially, the collision state and penetration depth) are transferred to the tactile hardware by the Tactile Data Transmitter (TDT). The TDT makes use of Bluetooth communication hardware embedded in the PDA.

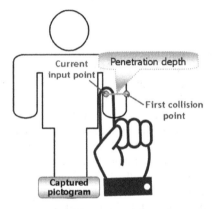

Fig. 4. Collision depth for actuating intensity of pager motors

3.2 Tactile User Interface and Low Level Control

This scenario requires a compact tactile hardware configuration suitable for a wearable environment. To realize this we designed a small and effective prototype tactile user interface. The tactile user interface is composed of two parts: the electric circuit and actuators. It is embedded in a glove like case, shown in Figure 5 (a). The actuators used are the coin type pager motors widely deployed in cell phones as they are relatively ergonomic and comfortable for the user. They have the additional qualities of being small, light, cheap and low in power consumption. To display a range of touch sensations, we used five vibrating actuators attached along and around the user's fingertip. Due to the limited resolution of the tactile display, it was important to carefully select the actuator sites. Since collisions between the user's fingertip and the pictogram will occur in response to directional movements, we choose to situate the tactile actuators so they provide directional information: on the left, right, front, back and center on the finger tip, as shown in Figure 5 (b). In order to more accurately

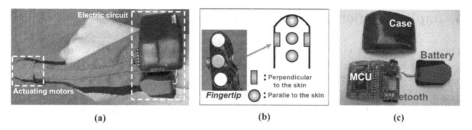

(a)   (b)   (c)

Fig. 5. (a) Glove type tactile interface, (b) Attached location of vibrating actuators, (c) Control hardware configuration

display the collision results with this tactile display, we differentiated among ten levels of collision depth each of which corresponded to a different intensity of vibration. To achieve this, the control hardware generated the control signal under a PWM (Pulse Width Modulation) paradigm with a duty ratio from 10% to 90%. These variations in duty ratio caused the actuators to emit vibrations of differing intensities.

This embedded system was implemented on an ATMega128 micro-controller unit (MCU) [36]. This is sufficiently small that it can be placed within in a glove type tactile interface while ensuring that it remains easily portable, as shown in Figure 5 (c). To generate the PWM signal with ten different intensities, we devised an algorithm which relies on the using system clock of the micro-controller. The micro-controller supports two 16-bit timer/counter units that allow accurate program execution timing, wave generation, and signal timing measurement. The PWM waveform is generated in a timer interrupt routine, and the PWM frequency for the output can be calculated by

$$f_{desire} = \frac{f_{system}}{2 \times N \times Count} \tag{1}$$

Where f_{sysem} represents the system frequency of the MCU up to 16MHz and N stands for the prescaler divider (1, 8, 64, 256, or 1024). **Count** represents the count number. The actual timer/count start value (2^{16}- **Count**) is calculated by equation (1) and then written in the count register of the MCU. This counter simply increases the start value until it reaches the top value (2^{16}) then begins again. For example, if the system frequency, the prescaler divider and the desired frequency are 16 MHz, 64 and 1 KHz, respectively, then the start number is 250. Accordingly the start value (2^{16}-250) is written to the count register. Consequently, a 1 KHz (with 50% duty cycle) waveform output is displayed. The duty ratio of the PWM waveform can be changed by manipulating the start value of timer/count register. The start value can be calculated by

$$Value_{bottom} = 2^{16} - (\frac{f_{system}}{f_{desire}} \times \frac{Duty}{100}) \tag{2}$$

With equation (2), the actuating intensity of the vibrating motors can not only be adjusted, but also controlled independently.

4 Implementation and Demonstration

The proposed tactile visualization system was implemented on an iPAQ hx4700 PDA (equipped with Intel's XScale PXA270 processor, an add on SDIO camera, and embedded Bluetooth 1.2) [37]. The Tactile User Interface (TUI) and the glove type interface were designed and built in house and are shown in Figure 4. To demonstrate the proposed system, we conducted an experiment by attaching specific pictograms to the walls of our laboratory. Figure 6 shows the pictogram representing a rest room appearing for tactile visualization in our mobile system.

In this demonstration, when user's fingertip wearing the tactile user interface collided with the pictogram, a collision response was calculated and transmitted to the tactile display hardware attached to glove type tactile user interface. This system achieves an overall performance of between 15 and 20 frames per second (fps). Although this is slow when compared with what can be achieved using a conventional computer, we expect that the power of wearable computing platforms will soon improve and evolve. In the case of the tactile display, the user experiences a range of vibrations delivered to their fingertip. Each tactile actuator is activated in response to a collision between the pictogram and the interaction point of the PDA's touch screen. If the user's finger moves deeper into the pictogram, the intensity of vibration is increased using the low level PWM control algorithm. This mechanism was primarily intended to provide the user with more detailed touch feedback. Therefore, users are able to recognize the collision depth as well as an edge of the pictogram were relative ease.

Fig. 6. Demonstration of the proposed tactile visualization system

5 Conclusions and Future Works

In this paper, we propose a system which combines tactile visualization with mobile augmented reality (AR) technology on a handheld device. To demonstrate and explore this system, we devised an application scenario based on helping visually impaired users to recognize specific pictograms or signs in the environment. For ensuring the pictogram detection and processing can take place in real time and without any pre-computation, we developed a component-based software architecture to accelerate the task of developing applications on a handheld device. In addition, the proposed system uses small-scale image processing based on RGB space of the captured pictogram in order to provide users with responsive touch interaction through their fingertip. We also have developed low level control methodologies for the vibrating actuators which allow users to experience more versatile tactile feedback. We predict this will assist a user in the task of recognizing shapes when touching captured pictograms. In conclusion, we expect that the proposed system will allow visually impaired users to recognize distributed pictograms existing in the real world and will encourage the development of various applications which feature wearable tactile interaction.

The next phase of this work is to conduct a comprehensive user study in which we evaluate the performance of visually impaired users with our system. This will determine the feasibility of our ideas. In addition, we will design new tactile pictograms which are easier to interpret with the tactile interface than those we are currently using. Furthermore, we will work to extend our system to other application areas and develop further interactive experiences in mobile environments. We are also interested in developing a more comprehensive tactile display algorithm to support more delicate sensations. Finally, in the long term, we hope to extend this work into outdoor environments to fully support a mobile experience in the broadest sense of the term.

Acknowledgment

This work was supported by the CTI development project, MCT and KOCCA in Korea and by the Ministry of Information and Communication through the Realistic Broadcasting IT Research Center (RBRC) at GIST.

References

1. Starner, T., Mann, S., Rhodes, B., Levine, J., Healey, J., Kirsch, D., Picard, R., Pentland, A.: Augmented Reality through Wearable Computing. Presence 6(4), 386–398 (1997)
2. Feiner, S., MacIntyre, B., Hoellerer, T.: Wearing it out: First steps toward mobile augmented reality systems. In: Proc. ISMR 1999. Int. Symp. on Mixed Reality, pp. 363–377 (1999)
3. Sato, K., Ban, Y., Chihara, K.: MR Aided Engineering: Inspection Support Systems Integrating Virtual Instruments and Process Control. In: Mixed Reality, pp. 347–362 (1999)
4. McGarrity, E., Genc, Y., Tuceryan, M., Owen, C., Navab, N.: Taking ar into large scale industrial environments: Navigation and information access with mobile computers. In: Proc. ISAR 2001. IEEE and ACM Int. Symp. on Augmented Reality, pp. 179–180. IEEE Computer Society Press, Los Alamitos (2001)
5. Klinker, G., Creighton, O., Dutoit, A.H., Kobylinski, R., Vilsmeier, C., Brügge, B.: Augmented maintenance of powerplants: a prototyping case study of a mobile AR system. In: Proc. ISAR 2001. IEEE and ACM Int. Symp. on Augmented Reality, pp. 124–133. IEEE Computer Society Press, Los Alamitos (2001)

6. Loomis, J., Golledge, R., Klatzky, R.: Personal Guidance System for the Visually Impaired Using GPS, GIS, and VR technologies. In: Proc. of Conf. on Virtual Reality System and Persons with Disabilities (1993)
7. Petrie, H., Johnson, V., Strothotte, T., Fritz, S., Michel, R., Raab, A.: MoBIC: Designing a Travel Aid for Blind and Elderly People. Journal of Navigation 49(1), 45–52 (1996)
8. Furmanski, C., Azuma, R., Daily, M.: Augmented-reality visualizations guided by cognition: Perceptual heuristics for combining visible and obscured information. In: Proc. ISMAR 2002. IEEE and ACM Int. Symp. on Mixed and Augmented Reality, pp. 215–224. IEEE Computer Society Press, Los Alamitos (2002)
9. Feiner, S., MacIntyre, B., Hollerer, T., Webster, A.: A touring machine: Prototyping 3D mobile augmented reality systems for exploring the urban environment. In: Proc. of the First IEEE Int. Symp. on Wearable Computers, pp. 74–81. IEEE Computer Society Press, Los Alamitos (1997)
10. Cheverst, K., Davies, N., Mitchell, K., Friday, A., Efstratiou, C.: Developing a Context-Aware Electronic Tourist Guide: Some Issues and Experiences. In: Proc. of ACM CHI 2000, ACM Press, New York (2000)
11. Fenier, S.: Augmented Reality: A New Way of Seeing. Scientific American 286(4), 48–55 (2002)
12. Hollerer, T., Pavlik, J.V., Feiner, S.: Situated documentaries: Embedding multimedia presentations in the real world. In: Proc. of The Third Int. Symp. on Wearable Computers, pp. 79–86 (1999)
13. Vlahakis, V., Ioannidis, N., Karigiannis, J., Tsotros, M., Gounaris, M., Stricker, D., Gleue, T., Daehne, P., Almeida, L.: Archeoguide: An Augmented Reality Guide for Archaeological Sites. IEEE Computer Graphics and Applications 22(5), 52–60 (2002)
14. Rekimoto, J., Ayatsuka, Y., Hayashi, K.: Augment-able reality: Situated communication through physical and digital spaces. In: Proc. ISWC 1998. Second Int. Symp. on Wearable Computers, pp. 68–75 (1998)
15. Baillot, Y., Brown, D., Julier, S.: Authoring of physical models using mobile computers. In: Proc. ISWC 2001. Fifth IEEE Int. Symp. on Wearable Computers, pp. 39–46. IEEE Computer Society Press, Los Alamitos (2001)
16. Piekarski, W., Thomas,B.: Tinmith-Metro: New outdoor techniques for creating city 16models with an augmented reality wearable computer. In: Proc. ISWC 2001. Fifth IEEE Int. Symp. on Wearable Computers, pp. 31-38, 2001.
17. Thomas, B., Close, B., Donoghue, J., Squires, J., De Bondi, P., Morris, M., Piekarski, W.: ARQuake: An outdoor/indoor augmented reality first person application. In: ISWC 2000. Fourth Int. Symp. on Wearable Computers, pp. 139–146 (2000)
18. Starner, T., Leibe, B., Singletary, B., Pair, J.: MIND-WARPING: towards creating a compelling collaborative augmented reality game. In: Proc. IUI 2000. Int. Conf. on Intelligent User Interfaces, pp. 256–259 (2000)
19. Fuchs, H., Livingston, M.A., Raskar, R., Colucci, D., Keller, K., State, A., Crawford, J.R., Radeacher, P., Drake, S.H., Meyer, A.: Augmented reality visualization for laparoscopic surgery. In: Proc. of the First Int. Conf. on Medical Image Computing and Computer-Assisted Intervention, pp. 934–943 (1998)
20. Salisbury, K., Barbagli, F., Conti, F.: Haptic Rendering: Introductory Concepts. IEEE Computer Graphics and Applications 24(2), 24–32 (2004)
21. Fritz, J.P., Way, T.P., Barner, K.E.: Haptic Representation of Scientific Data for Visually Impaired or Blind Persons. In: Proc. Annual Technology and Persons with Disabilities Conference (1996)

22. Fritz, J.P., Barner, K.E.: Design of a Haptic Visualization System for People with Visual Impairments. IEEE Transactions on Rehabilitation Engineering 7(3), 372–384 (1999)
23. Suthakorn, J., Lee, S., Zhou, Y., Thomas, R., Choudhury, S., Chirikjian, G.S.: Comprehensive Access to Printed Materials. Proc. of IEEE ICRA 4, 3589–3594 (2002)
24. Yu, W., Guffie, K., Brewster, S.A.: Image to Haptic Data Conversion: A First Step to Improving Blind People's Accessibility to Printed Graphs. In: Int. Conf. on Eurohaptics 2001, pp. 87–89 (2001)
25. Morris, D., Joshi, N.: Alternative Vision: A Haptic and Auditory Assistive Device. In: Proc. ACM SIGCHI Extended Abstracts, pp. 966–967. ACM Press, New York (2003)
26. Tan, H.Z., Gray, R., Young, J.J., Traylor, R.: A Haptic Back Display for Attentional and Directional Cueing. Haptics-e 3 (2003), http://www.haptics-e.org
27. van Erp, J., van Veen, H.: A Multi-purpose Tactile Vest for Astronauts in the International Space Station. In: Int. Conf. Eurohaptics 2003, pp. 405–408 (2003)
28. Tan, H.Z., Pentland, A.: Tactual Display for Wearable Computing. In: Proc. Symp. on Wearable Computers, pp. 84–89 (1997)
29. Yanagida, Y., Kakia, M., Lindeman, R.W., Kume, Y., Tetsutani, N.: Vibrotactile Letter Reading using a Low-Resolution Tactor Array. In: Proc. Symp. on Haptic Interfaces for Virtual Environment and Teleoperator Systems, pp. 400–406 (2004)
30. Loomis, J.: Tactile letter recognition under different Modes of stimulus presentation. Perception & Psychophysics 16(2), 401–408 (1974)
31. Yanagida, Y., Kakita, M., Lindeman, R.W., Kume, Y., Tetsutani, N.: Vibrotactile Letter Reading Using a Low-Resolution Tactor Array. In: Proc. Symp. on Haptic Interfaces for Virtual Environment and Teleoperator Systems, pp. 400–406 (2004)
32. Yang, U., Jang, Y., Kim, G.J.: Designing a Vibro-Tactile Wear for Colse Range Interaction for VR-based Motion Training In: ICAT 2002. Int. Conf. on Artificial Reality and Telexistence, pp. 4–9 (2002)
33. Lee, B.C., Lee, J., Cha, J., Seo, C., Ryu, J.: Immersive Live Sports Experience with Vibrotactile Sensation. In: Costabile, M.F., Paternó, F. (eds.) INTERACT 2005. LNCS, vol. 3585, pp. 1042–1045. Springer, Heidelberg (2005)
34. OpenGL|ES, http://www.zeuscmd.com/
35. ARToolkt Plus, http://studierstube.icg.tu-graz.ac.at/
36. Micro-controller, ATmega128, http://www.atmel.com
37. iPAQ hx 4700, PDA, http://www.hp.com

Mobile Multi-actuator Tactile Displays

Eve Hoggan, Sohail Anwar, and Stephen A. Brewster

Glasgow Interactive Systems Group, Department of Computing Science
University of Glasgow, Glasgow, G12 8QQ, UK
{eve,stephen}@dcs.gla.ac.uk
www.tactons.org

Abstract. The potential of using the sense of touch to communicate information in mobile devices is receiving more attention because of the limitations of graphical displays in such situations. However, most applications only use a single actuator to present vibrotactile information. In an effort to create richer tactile feedback and mobile applications that make use of the entire hand and multiple fingers as opposed to a single fingertip, this paper presents the results of two experiments investigating the perception and application of multi-actuator tactile displays situated on a mobile device. The results of these experiments show that an identification rate of over 87% can be achieved when two dimensions of information are encoded in Tactons using rhythm and location. They also show that location produces 100% recognition rates when using actuators situated on the mobile device at the lower thumb, upper thumb, index finger and ring finger. This work demonstrates that it is possible to communicate information through four locations using multiple actuators situated on a mobile device when non-visual information is required.

Keywords: Multimodal Interaction, Haptic I/O, Tactile Icons (Tactons), Mobile Displays, Multi-Actuator Displays.

1 Introduction

Tactile displays for mobile devices are becoming an important area of research in multimodal interaction. Mobile devices like PDAs and smart phones are becoming ever more popular as they provide many of the conveniences of a desktop computer in a mobile setting. However, they can be much more difficult to use due to demands on visual attention and limited screen space. Although audio output has proven to be an effective feedback modality for mobile devices, it can sometimes be inappropriate or go unnoticed, especially in a noisy environment like a concert or train station, or in a situation where it would be socially improper for a mobile device to ring loudly e.g. in a library or business meeting. These devices already commonly incorporate a vibrotactile actuator but with only very simple feedback. The potential of using the sense of touch to communicate information from mobile devices has already generated a body of research exploring various techniques such as vibrotactile icons (Tactons), lateral skin stretch display platforms, wearable displays and haptic pens [4, 9, 10, 12]. This research has shown that the sense of touch is a powerful communication medium for

I. Oakley and S. Brewster (Eds.): HAID 2007, LNCS 4813, pp. 22–33, 2007.

mobile devices and that users can understand information encoded in the tactile modality. However, these applications tend to involve only a single actuator to present vibrotactile information. Given the promising results from existing research, it may be possible to increase the bandwidth of information by investigating the use of multiple actuators to present information.

Typically, humans are accustomed to performing exploratory or manipulation tasks by using their hands and fingers [8]. The sensitivity of the human hand is based on a multitude of receptors embedded inside the fingertips and we gain a rich understanding of the objects we hold and touch. State-of-the-art tactile feedback displays for mobile device users already ensure high feedback quality, but often only for a single-fingered display or for a display with multiple actuators positioned on the body.

In an effort to create tactile feedback and mobile applications that make use of the entire hand and multiple fingers as opposed to a single fingertip, this paper presents the results from two experiments investigating the perception and application of multi-actuator tactile displays situated on a mobile device.

In related work, with regard to the feedback provided by the multi-actuator display, the output was based on previous research findings in Tactons work [3]. Tactons are structured vibrotactile messages which can be used to communicate information non-visually. They are the tactile equivalent of audio and visual icons. Tactons have been designed to be used in situations where the display may be overloaded, limited or unavailable, and when audio cues are not appropriate. Research carried out by Brown [4] showed that Tactons are effective as a means of communication and that by combining parameters like rhythm, spatial location and roughness, several dimensions of information can be presented to the sense of touch. The spatial locations used in Tactons research were on the forearm of mobile device users. This research will develop the spatial location parameter further by using positions on the actual device as opposed to positions on the user.

2 The Multi-actuator Mobile Device

We attached 4 EAI C2 Tactors (www.eaiinfo.com) to a standard PDA to provide vibrotactile feedback. Due to the number of C2 actuators required on the PDA to carry out the experiment, it was not possible to simply attach them to a PDA as this proved to be uncomfortable for the participants. Instead, the PDA was encased in a protective transparent cover and the actuators were embedded in the cover resulting in a more comfortable but still realistic experience (Fig. 1). Only the central part of the C2 vibrates, meaning that any vibration is localised and does not spread out across the whole device.

The C2 actuators were placed in four different positions on the PDA corresponding to locations on the hand: the lower thumb (bottom left side), the upper thumb (top left side), the tip of the index finger (top right on the back of the PDA) and the tip of the ring finger (middle right side). These locations were identified by observing how people held the PDA and where their hands made best contact with it. The actuators were controlled via a desktop PC using an M-Audio multi-out soundcard.

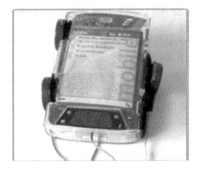

Fig. 1. The multi-actuator PDA used in experiment

3 Experiment 1 – Potential Locations on the Hand

The first experiment was conducted to evaluate the absolute identification of Tactons using two parameters: spatial location and rhythm. The aim of this experiment was to investigate the potential of using multiple locations on the same hand for tactile feedback from a mobile device, therefore providing data on how many and which of the locations would be effective. Headphones were worn by the participants to block out any residual sound from the device, to ensure that the participants were responding only to the tactile sensations and not to any audio leakage.

The set of Tactons used in this experiment consisted of three different rhythms (Fig. 2) with each of the four spatial locations. There were therefore 12 different Tactons presented 3 times to give 36 tasks in the experiment. Each lasted approximately 1 second and the rhythms used were based on those from Brown *et al.* [4].

Fig. 2. Two note, four note and six note rhythms used in the experiment (from [4])

Fifteen participants, all of whom were students at the University, took part in this experiment. Before beginning, all were given a tutorial to introduce the concepts of Tactons, rhythm, location, etc. Participants held the PDA in their non-dominant hand. In each task participants were presented with one Tacton and had to identify both attributes (the rhythm and the spatial location) encoded in it. They indicated their response by clicking on the corresponding radio buttons shown in Fig. 3. Once they had made their response they clicked the "Submit" button.

3.1 Results

During the experiment data were collected on the number of correct identifications of rhythm and location. Percentage correct scores were calculated for each individual dimension (rhythm and spatial location) and for the complete Tactons. To correctly

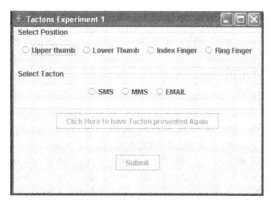

Fig. 3. Experiment location and rhythm selection experiment screenshot

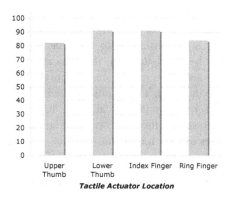

Fig. 4. Average percentage correct scores for each tactile actuator location

identify a complete Tacton, both of the individual dimensions had to be correctly identified. The average recognition rate for each location is shown in Fig. 4.

The average recognition rate for Tactons on the upper thumb was 82%, the ring finger 84% and 91% for both the lower thumb and index finger. Analysis of the data for each of the individual parameters (rhythm and location) showed that the average recognition rates for each location were 100%. No participant had a problem identifying the location of a Tacton. This result suggests that location on the hand is a very effective cue for a tactile display. The rhythm parameter was more difficult to identify and therefore reduced the overall Tacton recognition rates.

3.2 A Closer Look at Rhythm

The results of overall Tacton recognition showed an average recognition rate of 87.2%, with the 2-note rhythm having the highest recognition rate at 98.3% and the 6-note rhythm having the lowest at 81.6%. Table 1 shows the results for each rhythm, in the form of a confusion matrix which shows the number of times one stimulus was confused for another (as the location parameter got 100% recognition, no location was ever confused with another).

Table 1. Stimulus-response confusion matrix for rhythm

	2-Note Rhythm	4-Note Rhythm	6-Note Rhythm
2-Note Rhythm	98.3%	0.9%	0.8%
4-Note Rhythm	3.3%	83.3%	13.3%
6-Note Rhythm	0%	18.3%	81.6%

This shows that the participants experienced confusion attempting to distinguish between the 6-note Tacton and the 4-note one. There was rarely confusion between the 2-note Tacton and any other with the average recognition rate of 98.33% for the 2-note. The differences between each rhythm were investigated using a standard two-tailed one-factor ANOVA analysis. The results of the ANOVA indicate that there were no significant differences in error rates between three different rhythms with $F = 4.06$ where $p = 0.05$.

The results of this experiment indicate that spatial location using multiple actuators situated on the mobile device held in the non-dominant hand is an extremely effective parameter when transferring information to the hand (with identification rates of 100%). Therefore it can be concluded that these locations are able to successfully detect tactile information and these results are encouraging for further research in the transfer of information to the hand. The results for the individual locations are perfect and although the results for rhythm identification are lower, they are still comparable with results in previous research focusing on single actuator displays where Brown [5] found recognition rates of 93% for similar rhythms.

4   Experiment 2 – A More Realistic Application

Given the good results obtained in the first experiment, a second experiment was carried out involving multi-actuator tactile feedback in a more realistic application. As the multi-actuator set up allows more communication space, sensory saltation [7] could be used. The experiment conducted investigated the effectiveness of a tactile progress bar with error notification using a multi-actuator display.

4.1   Sensory Saltation

Sensory Saltation [7], also known as the 'Cutaneous Rabbit', usually involves three actuators placed at equal distances on the forearm, three brief pulses are delivered to

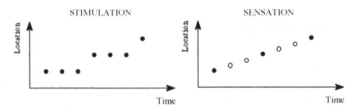

Fig. 5. Graphical representation of sensory saltation illusion [7]

the first actuator, followed by three more at the middle, followed by a final three at the last actuator. Instead of experiencing the successive stimulations as isolated events, the subject commonly feels that the pulses seem to be distributed with uniform spacing from the site of the first actuator to that of the third (Fig. 5). An important and useful feature of sensory saltation is the ability to simulate higher spatial resolution than the actual spacing of actuators. This has already been used successfully in wearable computing for applications such as directional cueing [12]. In this experiment, instead of using the forearm, the actuators are placed on the device held in the hand.

4.2 The Application

Progress bars are common and widely used to indicate the current state of a task which does not complete instantaneously, such as loading a Web page or copying files. However, there are a number of problems associated with such information when presented visually, for example, visual progress bars may become hidden behind other windows on the desktop and they must compete for screen space and visual attention with other visual tasks such as document editing or Web browsing. This problem is amplified on a mobile device such as a PDA or mobile phone due to the extremely limited screen space. In addition, the user may also need to concentrate on other tasks such as walking or navigating the environment whilst a potentially time consuming task takes place. Myers [11] showed that people prefer systems with progress indicators, as they give novices confidence that a task is progressing successfully whilst experts can get sufficient information to predict the approximate completion time of the task.

Research has already been conducted into the design of audio progress indicators, which give the user information about progress using non-speech sound, avoiding the problems of limited screen space. For example, Gaver [6] used the sound of liquid pouring from one container to another to indicate copying. However, such approaches have some drawbacks; for example, in a noisy environment cues may be missed, equally in a quiet environment the user may not wish to disturb others nearby. Previously research by Brewster and King [1] used Tactons to present progress information in desktop applications using a single actuator. They encoded the amount of download remaining in the time between two tactile pulses; the shorter the time between the pulses the less download remaining. The results of their experiment showed that users were able to detect completion of a download quicker via tactile means as compared

Fig. 6. Illusion of clockwise circular motion for a download, where black areas represent actuators on the PDA

to a visual progress bar, suggesting that a tactile display could also make a successful progress indicator for mobile applications.

The tactile progress bar used in our experiment was created to address the problems with visual progress bars by encoding progress information as a series of tactile cues which do not require visual attention and taking advantage of sensory saltation. This would give a greater perceived resolution to the progress indicator than using just a single actuator. A circular motion would be presented to the participant across three actuators (those at the lower thumb, upper thumb and the index finger), the speed of the motion indicating the rate of the download. In this case fast motion across the three actuators would indicate the download is progressing at high speed, slow motion indicating that the download is progressing at a slow speed.

The overall amount of progress was indicated by the rhythm of the vibration at each location, where a 6-note rhythm indicates that the download is in its early stages, 4-note rhythm indicates that a download is between 30% and 70% complete and a 2-note rhythm indicates that the download is nearing completion. Short simultaneous vibrations at each actuator were used to indicate task completion.

By using a multi-actuator display, the tactile space is greater than in previous single-actuator studies. Only three actuators were used for displaying the download, leaving one for another task. To mimic more realistic situations where a user might be monitoring a download whilst doing some other task, alongside the tactile progress bar we included a text entry task using a typical PDA on-screen keyboard. Here the fourth actuator (on the ring finger) would provide feedback on keyboard 'slips' in the form of a long vibration of 2 secs. duration. This allowed the investigation of the effectiveness of presenting two different forms of feedback via simple vibrotactile means across four actuators. Therefore, the primary task of participants in this experiment was text entry while progress information and information on slips was presented via tactile feedback.

A 'slip' in terms of this application is defined to be a condition where the user taps down on a particular keyboard button with the stylus but, due to some external force or misguided movement, the stylus slips from that button to another before the stylus is lifted, causing either the entry of an incorrect character or no character at all (see Brewster [2] or a more detailed discussion of slips). This is a common error in mobile settings where the movement of the user and device whilst walking can cause slip errors. They are often hard to identify via the visual feedback from the buttons so tactile feedback may help users notice that an error has been made.

4.3 Aim and Hypotheses

The aim of this experiment was to investigate a more realistic application for multi-actuator tactile displays than Experiment 1. This allowed us to assess the effects of tactile feedback at multiple locations on the mobile device in a more realistic scenario, and to see if the 100% recognition of locations observed in the initial experiment occurred again. The hypotheses were as follows:

1. Participants will be able to detect completion of downloads quicker with tactile feedback than a standard visual progress bar;
2. Participants will find it easier to detect slip errors when using the application with simple tactile feedback, as opposed to no tactile feedback;

3. Participants will experience reduced subjective workload due to the inclusion of tactile feedback;
4. Participants will not find masking to be a problem, as although it is likely to occur, it is unlikely to cause confusion due the large differences between the tactile feedback for progress information and the tactile slip error information.

4.4 Experimental Design and Procedure

Eight participants took part in the experiment, all students at the University. The experiment was a four condition within subjects design. The independent variable being the type of interface, giving four conditions to the experiment:

1. Standard visual feedback for slips and a visual progress bar;
2. Standard visual feedback for slips and tactile progress bar;
3. Tactile feedback for slips and a visual progress bar;
4. Tactile feedback for slips and tactile progress bar.

Data were recorded on the time taken to respond to the completion of a download (from when a download ended to when the participant clicked "Finished?" to indicate they had noticed its completion), the number of slip errors which remained undetected at the end of the condition, and subjective workload experienced (NASA TLX) in each condition.

The experimental tasks simulated typical mobile computing situations, where the user had to type text (in this case the text used was a poem) and monitor file downloads at the same time. The tasks involved entering as much text as possible in the time given whilst minimising errors and also monitoring the progress of the current download, detecting the completion of a download and pressing the "Finished?" button, which would initiate the next download (see Fig. 7). In total, each participant was presented with five downloads per condition, where the durations were randomly selected. Each participant was allowed four minutes per interface to enter text. The participants were also permitted a five-minute training period to become comfortable with the tactile feedback at the beginning of the experiment.

Fig. 7. Display for tactile progress information

4.5 Results

The results for the mean response times to download completion for each type of interface are shown in Fig. 8. This being the time from completion of the download to when the user clicked finished. Where:

- Interface 1 - no feedback for slips and a visual progress bar
- Interface 2 – no feedback for slips and a tactile progress bar
- Interface 3 - tactile feedback for slips and a visual progress bar
- Interface 4 - tactile feedback for slips and tactile progress bar

The results indicate that the participants responded faster to the completion of downloads when using the tactile progress bar. A one-factor ANOVA was used to investigate the significance of the effect. The result shows that the differences are significant (F = 2.95) To identify where differences lay, Tukey's HSD tests were carried out on the data. The results of the show that there was a significant difference (p=0.05) between mean response times for the interfaces which used a tactile progress bar and the interfaces which used a visual progress one (with no differences within the two tactile or visual conditions).

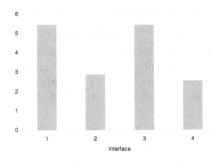

Fig. 8. Mean times to respond to end of downloads

This experiment incorporated text entry as the participants' primary task in which two of the interfaces provided tactile slip error information. The average number of slip errors undetected when using each interface is shown in Fig. 9. A one-factor ANOVA showed a significant effect (F= 2.94 with p = 0.05).

This shows that less slip errors were left undetected by participants when using the interface with tactile slip error feedback. There was no difference in the average number of undetected errors which remained after using the interface that provided

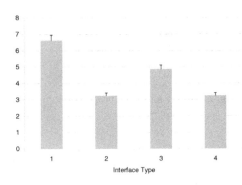

Fig. 9. Average number of undetected slip errors

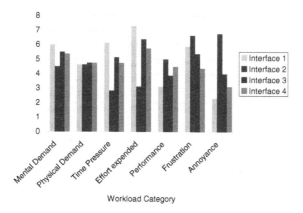

Workload Category

Fig. 10. NASA TLX responses

only tactile slip errors and the interface which provided both tactile progress and tactile slip error information.

As the results of the TLX workload assessments show (see Fig. 10), in the case where the participant was presented with only visual slip error information the participant experienced more frustration and annoyance while the least frustration was experienced using tactile feedback for both the progress bar and slips. However any differences were not found to be statistically significant as F = 2.5 where F crit = 3.23.

We are able to conclude that when using this particular tactile progress bar, participants were able to detect the completion of downloads faster than with the standard visual counterpart, this proves hypothesis one correct. This also confirms the result found by Brewster and King in their experiment [1].

The graph in Fig. 9 shows that the participants were not only able to detect more slip errors with tactile feedback but were able to do so just as effectively when being presented this at the same time as the tactile progress information, this proves hypothesis two correct and four, partly, correct. Although we can see differences in the workload experienced by participants when using each interface, by the mean comparison in **Fig. 10**, it was not the case that the participants experienced a reduced subjective workload by the inclusion of tactile stimuli, proving hypothesis 3 incorrect. The workload experienced was comparable to that of a standard visual based interface, this is a good basis for the introduction of tactile interfaces such as these.

The results of the statistical analysis confirm that the differences in response times to detection of completion of a download between tactile and visual interfaces were statistically significant. It also confirmed that the number of undetected slip errors showed a difference between interfaces, between the interfaces which incorporated slip information and those which did not. It was also found that less undetected errors remained after use of the interface which presented tactile progress information only. This is most likely due to the fact that the reduced effort required to monitor downloads allowed the participant to concentrate on ensuring fewer errors remained.

5 Conclusions

This paper presented two experiments investigating absolute identification of Tactons through a multi-actuator mobile device with a focus on potential locations on the hand to which vibrotactile information can be transferred successfully and potential applications of this technology. The results of these experiments show that an identification rate of over 87% can be achieved when two dimensions of information are encoded in Tactons using rhythm and location. They also show that location produces 100% recognition rates when using actuators situated on the mobile device at the lower thumb, upper thumb, index finger and ring finger.

The application presented in this paper is the use of Tactons presented by a mobile multi-actuator device in a tactile progress bar and in text entry error detection. Another possible application would be a waypoint navigation system. Previous work was discussed where an array of actuators was placed on a user's back [12] to provide directional information. This is not always a feasible solution as a special vest must be worn against the skin. A good alternative would be locations presented on the hand via a handheld device. This would allow a user with a PDA (or other mobile, perhaps dedicated, device) containing multiple actuators to navigate to a destination with little or no visual attention required on the mobile device.

In order to make use of multi-actuator displays in real mobile usage, future work will consider the presentation of vibrotactile information in a more realistic mobile setting, as identification may be affected by being engaged in another activity such as walking or exercising. We have refined our prototype so that it can now run from a laptop, soundcard and portable amplifier so that it now possible to use it on the move so we can investigate the effects of mobility. With further refinements we will be able to make the device self-contained.

In conclusion, this work has shown that it is possible to communicate information through four locations on the hand using multiple actuators situated on a mobile device. This is a significant step forward over single actuator displays as it now allows us to make use of the spatial dimension of tactile feedback in a convenient way. Multiple vibrotactile actuators no longer need to be built into jackets, belts, etc. which are hard to wear; they can be placed on the actual mobile device and carried by the user. We now have at least four locations available on the hand which presents a huge tactile space for many potential applications.

Acknowledgements

This work was funded by EPSRC Advanced Research Fellowship GR/S53244. Hoggan is joint-funded by Nokia and EPSRC.

References

[1] Brewster, S., King, A.: The Design and Evaluation of a Vibrotactile Progress Bar. In: Proc. First Joint Eurohaptics Conference and Symposium on Haptic Interfaces for Virtual Environment and Teleoperator Systems, pp. 499–500. IEEE Computer Society, Los Alamitos (2005)

[2] Brewster, S.A.: Overcoming the Lack of Screen Space on Mobile Computers. Personal and Ubiquitous Computing 6(3), 188–205 (2002)

[3] Brewster, S.A., Brown, L.M.: Tactons: Structured Tactile Messages for Non-Visual Information Display. In: Proc AUI Conference 2004, pp. 15–23. ACS (2004)

[4] Brown, L.M., Brewster, S.A.: Multidimensional Tactons for Non-Visual Information Display in Mobile Devices. In: Proc. MobileHCI 2006, pp. 231–238. ACM Press, New York (2006)

[5] Brown, L.M., Brewster, S.A., Purchase, H.C.: A First Investigation into the Effectiveness of Tactons. In: Proc. WorldHaptics 2005, pp. 167–176. IEEE Computer Society Press, Los Alamitos (2005)

[6] Gaver, W.: The SonicFinder: An Interface that Uses Auditory Icons. Human Computer Interaction 4(1), 67–94 (1989)

[7] Geldard, F.A.: Sensory Saltation: Metastability in the Perceptual World. Lawrence Erlbaum Associates, New Jersey (1975)

[8] Kron, A., Schmidt, G.: Multi-Fingered Tactile Feedback from Virtual and Remote Environments. In: Proc. 11th Symposium on Haptic Interfaces for Virtual Environment and Teleoperators, p. 16. IEEE Computer Society Press, Los Alamitos (2003)

[9] Lee, J.C., Dietz, P.H., Leigh, D., Yerazunis, W.S., Hudson, S.E.: Haptic pen: a tactile feedback stylus for touch screens. In: Proc. 17th annual ACM symposium on User interface software and technology, pp. 291–294. ACM Press, New York (2004)

[10] Luk, J., Pasquero, J., Little, S., MacLean, K., Levesque, V., Hayward, V.: A role for haptics in mobile interaction: initial design using a handheld tactile display prototype. In: Proc. SIGCHI conference on Human Factors in computing systems, pp. 171–180. ACM Press, New York (2006)

[11] Myers, B.A.: The Importance of Percent-Done Progress Indicators for Computer-Human Interfaces. In: Proc. SIGCHI conference on Human Factors in Computing Systems, pp. 11–17. ACM Press, New York (1985)

[12] Tan, H.Z., Pentland, A.: Tactual Displays for Wearable Computing. In: Proc the 1st IEEE International Symposium on Wearable Computers, pp. 84–89. IEEE Computer Society Press, Los Alamitos (1997)

Comparison of Force, Tactile and Vibrotactile Feedback for Texture Representation Using a Combined Haptic Feedback Interface

Ki-Uk Kyung, Jun-Young Lee, and Jun-Seok Park

POST-PC Research Group, Electronics and Telecommunication Research Institute
161 Gajeong-dong, Yuseong-gu, Daejeon, 305-700, Republic of Korea
{kyungku,dozob,parkjs}@etri.re.kr

Abstract. In this paper, we compared force feedback, tactile feedback and vibration feedback for texture display. For this investigation, a pen-like haptic interface with a built-in compact tactile display and a vibrating module was developed. The handle of pen held haptic interface was replaced by the pen-like interface to add tactile feedback capability to the device. Since the system provides combination of force and tactile feedback, three haptic representation methods have been compared on surface with 3 texture groups which differ in direction, groove width and shape. Over all the tests, the haptic device with combined with the built-in compact tactile display showed satisfactory results. Vibration feedback was also reasonably effective in texture display. From the series of experiments, applicability of the compact tactile display and usability of pen-like haptic interface in a pen held hapic interface have been verified.

Keywords: texture, combination, force, tactile, vibration.

1 Introduction

Researchers have proposed a diverse range of haptic interfaces. Force feedback devices, which have attracted the most attention with their capacity to convey physical forces to a user's body, have been applied to game interfaces, medical simulators, training simulators, and interactive design software, among other domains. However, compared to force feedback interfaces, tactile displays have not been deeply studied. This is at least partly due to the fact that the miniaturization necessary to construct such systems requires more advanced electronic and mechanical components. Moreover, development of a fast, strong, small, silent, safe tactile display module, with low heat dissipation and power consumption will allow the development of a haptic device providing combined force and tactile feedback.

We can imagine a haptic device providing both force and tactile feedback simultaneously. However, this kind of device requires a compact tactile display since the tactile display should be attached to the handle part of the force feedback device. Since Kontarinis *et al.* applied vibration feedback to a teleoperation in 1995 [5], some research works have had interests in combination of force and tactile feedback. Akamatsu *et al.* [1] suggested a computer mouse with tactile and force feedback

I. Oakley and S. Brewster (Eds.): HAID 2007, LNCS 4813, pp. 34–43, 2007.

increased usability. In 2004, Kammermeier *et al.* combined a tactile actuator array providing spatially distributed tactile shape display on a single fingertip with a single-fingered kinesthetic display and verified its usability[3]. However, the size of the tactile display was not small enough to practically use the suggested mechanism. As more practical design, Okamura and her colleagues design a 2D tactile slip display and installed it into the handle of a force feedback device [10]. Recently, in order to provide texture sensation with precisely controlled force feedback, a mouse fixed on 2DOF mechanism was suggested [6]. A small pin-array tactile display was embedded into a mouse body and it realized texture display with force feedback. The tactile display itself is quite small but its power controller is too big to be used practically. Our work in this paper deals with this issue as one of applications of our system.

In this paper, we compared force feedback, tactile feedback and vibration feedback for texture display. For this investigation, a pen-like haptic interface with a built-in compact tactile display and a vibrating module was developed. In section 2, the implementation of a pen-like haptic interface, we term the 'Ubi-Pen', including a tactile display module and vibrating motor is presented. In section 3, performance of a force and tactile feedback interface adopting the suggested pen-like interface is described. In particular, we compared three representation methods mentioned above. Finally, in section 4, we discuss possible applications of the proposed system including image display on a touch screen.

2 Ubi-Pen: Pen-Like Haptic Interface with Texture and Vibrotactile Display

In order to make a small tactile display, the actuator should be small, light, safe, silent, fast, strong, consume modest amounts of power and emit little heat. And the size of mechanism should be minimized to be embedded into a small portable device or into the handle of a force feedback device. With this point of view, we developed a prototype of very small tactile display module which has 3x3 pin array[7]. Since the actuators of the tactile display operate in the ultrasonic range, they produce little audible noise. The average thrusting force of each actuator exceeds 0.2N, sufficient to deform the skin with an indentation of 1 mm. The total size of the module is 12x12x12 mm and its weight is 2.5grams. The bandwidth of the tactile display is approximately 20Hz when used with a maximum normal displacement of 1mm.

The pen is a familiar device and interface. Since they are small, portable and easy to handle, styli have become common tools for interacting with mobile communication devices. In order to support richer stylus based tactile cues, we embedded our tactile display module into a pen-like prototype. In addition, we installed a pancake-type vibrating motor in the tip of the pen to provide a sense of contact (See Fig. 1). The housing of the pen was manufactured by rapid prototyping, and it has a length of 12cm and a weight of 15 grams. Currently, its controller is not embedded. We named this device the Ubi-Pen and intend it for use as an interface to VR, for the blind, to represent textures, and as a symbolic secure communication device.

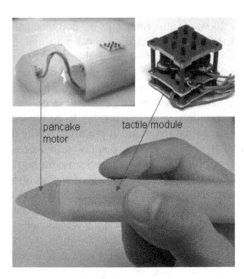

Fig. 1. The Prototype of the Ubi-Pen[7]. We embedded our tactile display module into a pen-like prototype and installed a pancake-type vibrating motor in the tip of the pen to provide a sense of contact.

3   Comparison of Force, Tactile, and Vibrotactile Feedback for Texture Representation

3.1   Force and Tactile Feedback Interface

Currently, the PHANToM^{TM} is the most widely used haptic interface. It has force feedback capabilities and it provides a stylus like handle interface [9]. Here we replace its handle with the Ubi-Pen to add tactile feedback capability to the device. Since the Ubi-Pen provides both vibration and texture stimuli, this allows us to compare the effectiveness of various haptic stimulation methods. As shown in Fig. 2, the proposed pen-like interface was attached to the handle of a force feedback device (Model: PHANToM Omni).

3.2   Methodology of Texture Representation

In order to test performance of the system, we designed a virtual environment including a box. The virtual object is a box and its stiffness is 2kN/m. (The task in this experiment does not require high interaction force.) The widths are 60 and 54 mm. The upper surface of the box has a texture derived from texture mapping an image. In order to use the image as a texture, this test provides a symbolic pointer in the shape of a square, with a size of 15x15 pixels. This scheme has been suggested in our previous work for the tactile display[7]. A user can load any grayscale image. As shown in Fig. 3, when the user touches an image on the box with the integrated interface, the area of the cursor is divided into 9(=3x3) sub-cells and the average gray value of each cell is calculated. Then, this averaged gray value is converted to the intensity of the stimuli displayed on each pin of the tactile display.

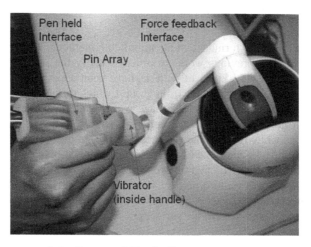

Fig. 2. The Prototype of the Force and Tactile Feedback Interface. The proposed pen-like interface was attached to the handle of a force feedback device.

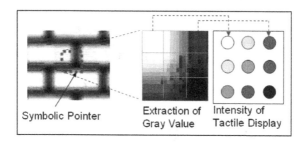

Fig. 3. Methodology of Pattern Display[7]. When the user touches an image on the box with the integrated interface, the area of the cursor is divided into 9(=3x3) sub-cells and the average gray value of each cell is calculated.

In this interaction, the stiffness of the box is represented by the PHANToM force feedback device. However, the texture on the surface can be represented in 3 ways. The first is through force feedback presented by the PHANToM since we can feel texture by probe scanning. The second is texture feedback by the Ubi-Pen since the pin's movement can display surface roughness. The third is the Ubi-Pen's vibration feedback since such stimuli could facilitate the recognition of obstacles when rubbing a surface. We compared all 3 possible stimulation methods in this experiment.

As mentioned above, the area of virtual cursor is divided into 9 cells each with an individual gray value. However, while the tactile display inside the pen interface has 9 spatially distributed stimulators, the vibrator and force feedback interface both have only one interaction point. Therefore force feedback and vibration feedback use only the center value.

In case of force feedback, the gray value is converted into the height of pattern and its highest value is 1 mm. In case of tactile feedback, the gray value is converted into the normal displacement of each pin and the maximum displacement is 1mm. The vibrator reflects gray values in the form of its intensity controlled by pulse width modulation.

3.3 Experimental Design

In order to compare the performance of all stimulation methods, we prepared 3 groups of tactile patterns. In a previous work, in order to verify the performance of tactile display on a touch screen, 3 kinds of patterns have been adopted as shown in Fig. 4 [8]. Fig. 4.(a) shows 5 image samples from group I which differ in the direction of the gratings they feature. The size of each image was 300x270 pixels. Fig. 4.(b) shows image samples from group II which contain grooves of varying widths. A user feels horizontal gratings while rubbing the surfaces. In order to discriminate these patterns, the tactile stimuli must be integrated with movements on the plane. Fig. 4.(c) shows 5 image samples from group III, each of which shows different shapes. Discriminating among these patterns will require precise and accurate integration of the tactile cues with the movements on the surface. Feeling distributed pressure (as with the pin array display) may help users to discern the surfaces.

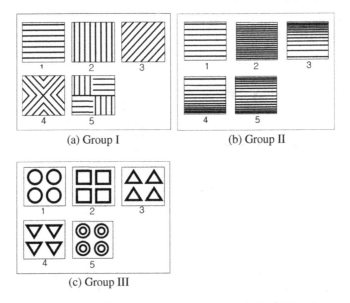

(a) Group I   (b) Group II

(c) Group III

Fig. 4. Texture Sample Groups. Three haptic representation methods have been compared on surface with 3 texture groups which differ in direction, groove width and shape.

10 subjects participated in the experiment. In each trial, one of the five images from one of the groups was texture-mapped on the upper surface of a virtual box. However, the graphical representation was hidden, and only a blank surface display. When the user touched and rubbed the surface of the object, the gray values of the image were conveyed to the haptic interface. They were then required to state which texture was present. All texture images in a group were presented 4 times at random and the order of test group was also randomly selected. The user felt the stiffness of the box by force feedback, but there were three conditions for representing texture: force feedback, tactile feedback and vibration feedback. In order to prevent practice

effects the order of the stimulation method was also randomized. Finally, sounds produced during the interaction may affect recognition performance so participants were required to wear noise cancelling headphones (Bose, QuietComfort2). Fig. 5 shows a participant is exploring the virtual environment with force and tactile feedback interface.

Fig. 5. Experimental Environment. A participant is exploring the virtual environment with force and tactile feedback interface.

3.4 Experimental Results and Discussion

Fig. 6 shows the average percentage of correct answers for all stimulation methods. Fig. 7 shows the mean durations of trials in each condition.

The texture samples assigned in group I can be discriminated by detecting the direction of the gratings. Users can recognize the direction from the position of the interaction point and the direction in which they rub. In this case, there is no substantial difference between force feedback and vibration feedback. However, tactile display provides line load to the finger along the gratings. As shown in Fig. 6 and Fig. 7, this makes human recognize direction of the gratings more correctly and quickly.

For group II, the images can be discriminated by the variations in the spacing between the ridges. However, the spatial resolution of the human arm is not sufficient to reliably detect variations on the scale of mm whereas the skin sense allows discrimination of sub mm gaps [2]. In addition, pattern display by force feedback inherently results in movement of the arm and even stick slip vibration, factors which may disturb discrimination of gap variation. Therefore, as shown in Fig. 6, the percentage of correct answers for force feedback is lower than in the other conditions. A good example is that users experienced difficulty discriminating between sample 2 and sample 5. (For sample 2, 22.5 percent of answers were sample 5.) In the case of the tactile feedback, the narrow gaps are discriminated though the skin. This shows the best performance. In the case of the vibration feedback, the participants typically rubbed the surface at a constant speed and felt the frequency of the vibrations. This technique was also effective.

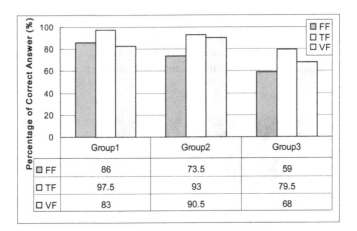

Fig. 6. Average Percentage of Correct Answers. The haptic device with combined with the built-in compact tactile display showed satisfactory results. Vibration feedback was also reasonably effective in texture display with force feedback.

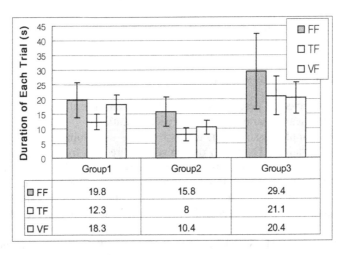

Fig. 7. Duration of Each Trial. These results shows the tactile feedback with force feedback is more effective than vibrotactile feedback with force feedback in group I and group II.

As mentioned in section 3.1, in order to recognize shape of a pattern, the tactile stimuli must be accurately integrated with movements on the plane. However, arm movements do not guarantee the high spatial resolution required for this. For example, when sample 1 was presented, users found it hard to discern it from the other samples. (Percentage of correct answers for sample 1 was only 44%. For sample 1, 15% of answers were sample 2, 22.5% were sample 3, and another 22.5% were sample 4.) But, in case of the tactile feedback, the distributed pressure cues enabled them to make more accurate choices.

If the tactile display had more pins, it might show better performance. However, over all the tests, the haptic device with combined with the built-in compact tactile display showed satisfactory results. Vibration feedback was also reasonably effective in texture display with force feedback.

4 Application

One of possible application of the combination of force and tactile feedback is a palpation medical simulator. Palpation is a kind of diagnosis based on pressure and pressure distribution. Therefore, when we develop a haptic palpation simulator, both force and tactile display interface is required. Kim *et al.* [4] proposed a palpation simulator based on this structure. However, their tactile display was somewhat cumbersome. The use of our tactile display or the Ubi-Pen might enhance the usability of this system. And there have been many other studies for haptic medical simulators those required a compact tactile display for more realistic and effective skin sense feedback.

Fig. 8. Interactive Haptic Drawing Program. When the user scratches the touch screen with the haptic stylus, the PC generates scratching sound varied by scratching speed and ground material. And the variation of image values while the stylus moves on the touch screen is reflected to the variation of vibration intensity of the haptic stylus.

This scheme mentioned in section 3.3 can be applied to educational programs for children or interactive drawing software as shown in Fig 8. The developing system is composed of a haptic stylus and a touch panel PC. If the background image is sand, the software provides users with sandplay-like experience. The haptic stylus plays a role of a drawing stick. When the user scratches the touch screen with the haptic stylus, the PC generates scratching sound varied by scratching speed and ground material. And the variation of image values while the stylus moves on the touch screen is reflected to the variation of vibration intensity of the haptic stylus. The only preliminary work had been conducted and now, we are trying to investigate a method to provide more precise tactile feeling.

One of the most practical uses of our compact tactile display is Braille display. In particular, it can realize a highly portable Braille display. However, we need to conduct more precise evaluations before construction such a system. Finally, the tactile display module could be installed in new interactive game simulator, education system or mobile communication devices.

5 Conclusion

In this paper, force feedback, tactile feedback and vibration feedback for texture display has been compared. For this investigation, a pen-like haptic interface with a built-in compact tactile display and a vibrating module was developed. The handle of pen held haptic interface was replaced by the pen-like interface to add tactile feedback capability to the device. Since the system provides combination of force and tactile feedback, three haptic representation methods have been compared on surface with 3 texture groups which differ in direction, groove width and shape. Over all the tests, the haptic device with combined with the built-in compact tactile display showed satisfactory results. Vibration feedback was also reasonably effective in texture display with force feedback.

As a future work, the Ubi-pen will be designed for multi purposes. For this, more compact tactile display will be developed and it may realize tactile display installed mobile communication device and a useful haptic stylus. And the performance of tactile feedback and vibrotactile feedback will be continuously compared and either of them will be able to be applied properly.

Acknowledgment

This work was supported by the IT R&D Program of MIC/IITA[2007-S032-01, Development of an Intelligent Service technology based on the Personal Life Log]. The authors appreciate Ian Oakley's kind comments and editing.

References

1. Akamatsu, M., MacKenzie, I.S.: Movement characteristics using a mouse with tactile and force feedback. International Journal of Human-Computer Studies 45, 483–493 (1996)
2. Johnson, K.O., Phillips, J.R.: Tactile spatial resolution. I. Two-point discrimination, gap detection, grating resolution, and letter recognition. Journal of Neurophysiology 46(6), 1177–1192 (1981)
3. Kammermeier, P., Kron, A., Hoogen, J., Schmidt, G.: Display of holistic haptic sensations by combined tactile and kinesthetic feedback. Presence-Teleoperators and Virtual Environments 13, 1–15 (2004)
4. Kim, S.Y, Kyung, K.U., Kwon, D.S., Park, J.: Real-time area-based haptic rendering and the augmented tactile display device for a palpation simulator. Advanced Robotics 21(9), 961–981 (2007)

5. Kontarinis, D.A., Howe, R.D.: Tactile display of vibratory information in teleoperation and virtual environments. Presence: Teleoperators and Virtual Environments 4(4), 387–402 (1995)
6. Kyung, K.U., Kwon, D.S., Yang, G.H.: A Novel Interactive Mouse System for Holistic Haptic Display in a Human-Computer Interface. International Journal of Human Computer Interaction 20(3), 247–270 (2006)
7. Kyung, K.U., Park, J.S.: Ubi-Pen: Development of a Compact Tactile Display Module and Its Application to a Haptic Stylus. In: Proc. of Worldhaptics Conference, pp. 109–104 (2007)
8. Kyung, K.U., Lee, J.Y., Park, J.S.: Pen-like Haptic Interface and Its Application on Touch Screen. In: Proc. of IEEE International Symposium on Robot and Human Interactive Communication, pp. 9–13 (2007)
9. Massie, T.H., Salisbury, J.K.: PHANTOM Haptic Interface: A Device for Probing Virtual Objects. In: Proc. of the ASME Winter Annual Meeting, Symposium on Haptic Interfaces for Virtual Environment and Teleoperator Systems, Chicago, IL (1994)
10. Webster, R.J., Murphy, T.E., Verner, L.N., Okamura, A.M.: A novel two-dimensional tactile slip display: design, kinematics and perceptual experiments. Transactions on Applied Perception (TAP) 2(2), 150–165 (2005)

Shake2Talk: Multimodal Messaging for Interpersonal Communication

Lorna M. Brown[1] and John Williamson[2]

[1] Microsoft Research, 7 JJ Thomson Ave, Cambridge CB3 0FB
lornab@microsoft.com
[2] Department of Computing Science, University of Glasgow, G12 8QQ
jhw@dcs.gla.ac.uk

Abstract. This paper explores the possibilities of using audio and haptics for interpersonal communication via mobile devices. Drawing on the literature on current messaging practises, a new concept for multimodal messaging has been designed and developed. The *Shake2Talk* system allows users to construct audio-tactile messages through simple gesture interactions, and send these messages to other people. Such messages could be used to communicate a range of meanings, from the practical (e.g. "home safely", represented by the sound and sensation of a key turning in a lock) to the emotional (e.g. "thinking of you" represented by a heartbeat). This paper presents the background to this work, the system design and implementation and a plan for evaluation.

Keywords: haptics, audio, vibrotactile, multimodal interaction, mobile phones, messaging, remote communication, gesture recognition.

1 Introduction

It has been reported that there may be a need for new genres of communication [1, 2]. Harper [1] observed that people wish to use a mix of communication channels rather than one single channel, giving the example that paper mail is still in use despite the introduction of email and instant messaging. It seems that there may still be more new ways in which people could communicate, and this research aims to explore new possibilities for mobile communication. Currently the main forms of mobile communication are voice calls, text messaging (SMS) and multimedia messaging (MMS). This research investigates the area of non-visual messaging, in particular messaging using non-speech audio and vibrotactile display.

Non-speech sound and touch are ubiquitous in our everyday lives, but their potential in remote technology-mediated communication has not yet been realized. Using non-visual modalities such as sound and touch offers new opportunities for mobile messaging. A user's eyes are often engaged in other tasks when a message arrives, and they cannot look away from their current activity to attend to it. In addition if they are engaged in a physical task (e.g. driving, cooking), they are unable to pick up the phone and interact with it to receive a message. If the message was a non-speech audio or a vibrotactile message, instead of a visual message, and was presented to the user upon arrival (rather than requiring that the user open the inbox to

I. Oakley and S. Brewster (Eds.): HAID 2007, LNCS 4813, pp. 44–55, 2007.

retrieve it), the user would be able to receive the information peripherally without having to disengage from their current activity to interact with the device.

Modalities such as non-speech audio and vibrotactile displays might offer new ways of communicating over and above text, speech, or picture messaging. It is said that a picture is worth a thousand words; could the same be true for a sound or a touch? A simple touch can have a much stronger impact than words, and sounds can evoke strong emotions and associations. It would be interesting to explore how people might communicate if they could send sounds or vibrotactile messages in place of, or in addition to, text or multimedia messages.

Based on these ideas, this paper presents a new concept for mobile messaging. The *Shake2Talk* system allows a user to create multimodal audio-tactile messages through simple gesture interactions with a mobile device, and then send these messages to another user. The long term aim of this research is to explore how such a non-visual, multimodal communication system might be used for interpersonal communication, alongside current messaging genres, when deployed with users. The paper presents a review of current messaging genres (Section 2) and related work on non-visual communication (Section 3), and then describes the Shake2Talk system, along with a plan for evaluation (Section 4).

2   Current Mobile Messaging Genres

In designing a new genre for communication it is important to consider the ways in which people currently communicate using mobile phones. The two main messaging genres are text messaging (SMS) and multimedia messaging (MMS) and a number of studies have investigated how people, particularly teenagers, use these services [3-7].

Ling, Julsrud and Ytrri [5] provide a categorization of the uses of text messaging. They state that the main uses are: co-ordination of events, questions, grooming (compliments/small talk), short one-word answers, commands/requests, information, personal news, invitations, jokes, thank you notes and apologies. Kopomaa [4] said that the main uses of SMS are for setting up meetings, exchanging gossip, giving info/reminders, and coordinating shared activities. Kasesniemi and Rautiainen [3] found that teenagers' use of SMS differs when they text their peers from when they text their family members. Between peers, teenagers use text messaging to express emotions, to gossip, to express longing, and to say things that they might not say in person, whereas, within a family group, they use text messaging for practical matters. SMS is also used within families to reinforce the family unit. The authors report the delight of a mother who received a message saying "mommy, I love you, I took out the garbage" from her 11 year old daughter in the middle of a work day [3].

Kindberg *et al.* [7] report a study of camera-phone use. They found that photo messaging was used for both emotional and functional purposes. The main uses were: extending an experience to absent friends, embodying personal common ground (e.g. sharing something that reminds you of a person, and which they will understand because of a shared history), as part of a conversation, to complete a task (e.g. sending images of an item of clothing to an absent person while shopping to ask if this is the item they want), conveying news, and providing evidence of an event (e.g. sending a photo when you arrive somewhere to show that you are there safely).

It will be interesting to see where a new form of messaging, such as audio-tactile messaging, might fit into these genres. Would it mainly be used for playful messaging, or might it also be used to provide information or commands/requests? Might it reveal new types of messaging that have previously not been used?

The literature on SMS shows that text messages are often treated like gifts [6]. They are carefully crafted by senders and often saved and treasured by recipients [2, 3]. Some of the literature on multimedia messaging indicates that the gift-like quality of messages is dependent on the effort put into crafting or creating the message by the sender [5]. This raises interesting questions for audio-tactile messaging. Will such messages also be treated as gifts? For them to be treated as gifts do they need to be crafted or constructed by the user? If so, does this mean that the user needs to record their own sounds and send them? Or would it be enough "craftsmanship" if the user created their own unique messages by interacting with a set of sounds and tactile sensations to create an audio-tactile message?

Another element that comes out of the literature on mobile phone use is that fiddling with objects, like beads, cigarettes, keys, etc seems to be a fundamental part of human nature, and a means of obtaining pleasure, and that fiddling with a mobile phone may also provide pleasure [4]. It might be possible to exploit this by using the fiddling with the phone itself to create messages, for example through gesture interaction, so that the fiddling itself actually becomes the means by which the message is created. This physical creation of the messages might also enable the craftsmanship required to create a message which would be considered to be a gift.

3 Non-visual Communication

In addition to considering the use of commercial messaging services, it is useful to consider related research in non-visual communication. This section discusses the use of touch and sound in real world and technology-mediated communication.

3.1 Communication Via Touch

Touch is widely used in social communication to enhance other forms of communication, and can "emphasize, qualify or contradict spoken words" [8]. Thayer [8] states that touch "will be trusted more by the person touched as a genuine reflection of feelings than all other forms of human communication". The literature also reports that "touching another's body generates an immediate demand for a response" [8], and that a lack of response may imply rejection [9]. Jones and Yarborough [9] grouped touch in social interaction into six categories: positive affect touches (support, appreciation, inclusion, sexual, affection), playful touches (playful affection, playful aggression), control touches (compliance, attention getting, announcing a response), ritualistic touches (greeting, departure), task related touches (reference to appearance, touch during a task) and accidental touches.

Considering the functions of touch in social communication may provide inspiration for the design of audio-tactile messages. The sense of touch is particularly interesting in remote communication since it is something that, currently, can only occur in face to face communication and not remotely. A touch of the hand can give reassurance; what if someone could send a "touch" to someone else's mobile phone to reassure them remotely? This does not necessarily mean that touch in face to face communication should be replaced in remote communication by mechanical touch but, rather, that the functions of social touching should be enabled through remote messaging. Therefore, the above categories of social touching may provide inspiration for the types of non-visual messages that people might want to send.

Vibrotactile displays, such as pager motors and other similar actuators are low-cost and widely available. Such displays are appropriate for communication systems as they are private to the user, and are attention grabbing. The disadvantage is that they need to be in contact with the skin for messages to be felt. A range of work has been conducted in the field of mediated social touch, both using vibrotactile display and tangible interfaces. A full review of this work is available from [10]. One such system is The Hug [11]: a robotic device which allows physical communication between two people. Hugging, stroking and squeezing a Hug device will send heat and vibrations to another Hug device. Other systems have been built to allow people to send vibrotactile messages via mobile phones [12] and instant messaging applications [13]. In recent work, Smith and MacLean [14] have explored the communication of emotion through a virtual hand stroke using a single degree of freedom haptic knob, with very promising results. Research has also been conducted into how to design complex vibrotactile messages for communicating rich data [15, 16]. However, it has been shown that, when these messages are abstract, training is needed, and the recognition rates are quite low [15]. Recognition rates are higher when tactile messages that use a metaphorical mapping to real world concepts are used, but the set of such messages is limited [16].

3.2 Communication Via Non-speech Audio

In the real world, we use sounds to understand what is going on around us, e.g. the sounds of doors opening and closing in our home or workplace indicate that people are arriving or leaving, the sound of pots and pans indicates that someone is cooking dinner, etc. In general, such peripheral awareness through sound is only available through co-location. If people could send sounds, then perhaps they could use this as a means to provide people with remote awareness of their actions. Audio display is widely available in mobile devices, with all mobile phones having audio output capabilities and many featuring high quality audio for their MP3 player functionality. The disadvantage of audio, compared to tactile display, is that it can be heard by other people, unless headphones are worn.

Two main forms of non-speech audio have been used in computer interfaces, Earcons and Auditory Icons. Earcons [17] are structured, abstract non-speech sounds, whereas Auditory Icons [18] use real world sounds to communicate information. Auditory Icons are of particular interest to this research since they use real world sounds with which users will already be familiar and, therefore, offer more opportunities for immediate expression without training to learn meanings.

Much of the research on non-speech audio display has focused on feedback on user actions and notification of system state rather than on communication. For example, Gaver's SonicFinder [18] used auditory icons to provide feedback on user interface events such as dragging, copying, opening or deleting files/folders. Earcons have also been used for feedback on system state and actions [17]. Gaver's [19] EARS (Environmental Audio Reminders) system used non-speech audio to support collaboration and awareness in a work environment. Auditory icons were presented to offices and common areas to remind people of meetings (the sound of murmuring voices) or to announce a trip to the pub (the sound of voices and of a beer being poured). In addition sounds were used to indicate emails arriving or people connecting to a video camera. All of this research has shown is that it is possible for people to attend to, and understand, non-speech sounds, while engaged in other tasks.

Some research has investigated the use of non speech audio for communication. For example, the Hubbub system [20] allowed people to send Sound Instant Messages (SIMs), in the form of Earcons, alongside text instant messages. In addition the system played sounds to indicate when contacts signed in or out, to provide peripheral awareness. Users could choose from a set of 14 pre-defined messages to send as SIMs. These SIMs were used quite regularly, but people found it hard to remember many different sounds. This might be improved by using auditory icons instead of Earcons, as people can then use their own real world associations to remember the messages. In addition, users might be more creative and expressive if they could interpret the sounds in their own way rather than having the meanings pre-assigned.

3.3 Discussion of Related Work on Non-visual Communication

This review has shown that both sound and touch are used regularly in real world communication and awareness, and there has been a range of work using these modalities for remote communication. However, many of these systems have a very limited vocabulary for communication. For example, squeezing or stroking an object to send a "hug" is very literal and offers little scope for new interpretations or new types of expression. Harper and Hodges [2] note that many remote communication applications "are popular at first, but soon wither: their value turning out to be essentially gimmicky and short-lived. Moreover, it also appears that they wither in part because what is communicated (and to some degree how) is sometimes too literal from the user perspective". They go on to say that, for a genre to succeed, it needs to be expressive rather than constrained, allowing users to communicate in rich ways [2]. This needs to be considered when designing any new communication genre. Whereas many of the systems described above have a single, literal function, e.g. squeezing an object to send a "hug", a system for richer communication needs to enable a wider range of messages to be sent, and to allow users to interpret these messages in their own ways. In so doing, it may be possible to open up a more open and less literal communication channel that allows new means of expression.

From this review of related work, a number of lessons can be learned for designing a new system for remote, interpersonal communication. The system should allow people to express themselves in rich ways, and should, therefore, offer a wide vocabulary and use messages that are open to interpretation by users rather than using very literal messages. Non-visual modalities, in particular non-speech real world audio and vibration, seem to offer promise for a new genre of communication. By building a non-visual communication system and deploying it with users it will be possible to investigate a number of questions, e.g. how do people communicate when using such a system, and how is it used alongside other forms of communication? One limitation of much of the previous work on non-visual communication is that there have not been any long term evaluations of the systems in use. The long term aim of this research is to deploy *Shake2Talk* in a longitudinal study, to understand how it is used alongside existing communication methods.

4   The Shake2Talk System

Based on the above discussion, a new concept has been generated for remote non-visual communication. *Shake2Talk* is a mobile audio-tactile messaging system. Audio-tactile messages are created by a user through simple gesture interactions with a mobile phone. After the message has been composed, the user presses send and the message is sent across the mobile phone network via SMS to the chosen recipient. Upon arrival the message is presented immediately (Figure 1). The reasons for these choices of input and output modalities are discussed further in the following sections.

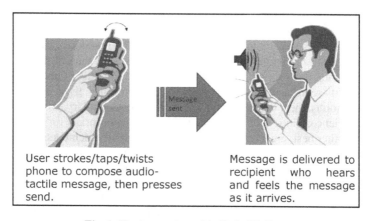

| User strokes/taps/twists phone to compose audio-tactile message, then presses send. | Message is delivered to recipient who hears and feels the message as it arrives. |

Fig. 1. The interaction with *Shake2Talk*

The *Shake2Talk* system comprises a Windows Smart Phone with a SHAKE device from SAMH Engineering fixed to the back of the phone (Figure 2). The SHAKE device contains inertial sensors (accelerometers, gyroscopes, capacitive sensors), which are used for gesture recognition. It also contains an eccentric-weighted pager motor to provide vibrotactile output (with control over onset, offset and frequency). The *Shake2Talk* application is run on the Smart Phone, which also provides audio output. The system is integrated with a mobile phone as it was felt that people would be more likely to adopt a system which works with their existing phone, than to carry a separate device. Although the SHAKE device is currently a separate unit, this could be integrated into the phone. Some phones contain accelerometers (e.g. Nokia 5500, Samsung SCH-310) and most feature vibration motors.

Fig. 2. The SHAKE device from SAMH Engineering, (left) and the SHAKE device attached to a smart phone and held by a user (right)

4.1 Output Modalities

Section 3 indicated that both audio and vibrotactile modalities offer a number of advantages and disadvantages. Tactile messages are private to the user and would not be overheard by others, but only a limited number of tactile messages can be identified, and training is necessary. By using audio messages it is possible to find a wider range of messages which can easily be interpreted by users. Real world sounds (auditory icons) could be particularly effective since people already have associations with such sounds. Whilst audio messages are not private to the user, it is possible that privacy regarding what is being communicated can be retained. The meaning of the audio message is likely not to be literal and, therefore, is probably only understandable to the parties to the communication. For example, whilst one couple might send a heartbeat sound to indicate that they are thinking of one another, another couple might send a heartbeat sound to indicate that they are nervous. The communication is, thus, dependent on a shared audio vocabulary, which results from a shared experience. Thus, such a system will be most appropriate for those people who know each other best, e.g. couples, close friends or family members. It should also be noted that people already use a range of sounds for personalized ringtones and, thus, there may be less concerns about phones producing sounds than one might expect.

Given the argument that audio offers a richer vocabulary than tactile, it might seem sensible to use audio-only messaging. However, by adding vibrotactile feedback to the audio, the information is redundantly coded in two modalities and the user will still feel the message whilst in a noisy environment. The tactile feedback also adds to the feeling of engagement when creating the message, and enhances the output. If distinctive tactile messages are used, they could be learned implicitly alongside the audio messages and then, eventually, could be used alone for discreet communication. Given these arguments, the final design for *Shake2Talk* uses non-speech everyday sounds, paired with synchronized tactile feedback (see Section 4.3 for further detail).

4.2 Inputs

A number of different input techniques could be used to select or create audio-tactile messages, with the most obvious being to select a preset message from a list. It might be more engaging for the user to interact directly with the audio and tactile feedback to create a message themselves. This can be done through gesture interaction with the device. In addition to providing engagement, it may be quicker for the user to perform a simple gesture (such as a tap, twist or a stroke) than to navigate through a series of menus to find the message. It was discussed in Section 2 that people fiddle with their phone to fill time, and it could be interesting to explore how such "fiddling", through gesture interaction, could be a means by which the messages are created. The element of "gift giving" in messaging may be partly dependent on the fact that the sender has taken time and effort to create the message. By having users create an audio-tactile message dynamically through gestures, these gift-like qualities may be retained more than if the user had simply selected a preset message from a list. Using gesture input may also lead to a very different experience than using menu input. In particular it results in an asymmetry between the experience of the sender and the experience of the recipient. When menu selection input is used, the sender and the recipient both experience the message passively. When gesture input is used, the sender actively interacts with the sounds and vibrations, whereas the recipient's experience is passive. It will be interesting to investigate whether this asymmetry of experience affects the perception of the meaning of the messages. *Shake2Talk* has been designed with both input options (menu selection and gesture input) so that they can be evaluated and compared.

Table 1. The Four Types of Gesture used in Shake2Talk

Gesture	Recognition
Stroke: User slides a finger from one capacitive sensor to the other in a "stroking" motion.	Recognition is performed by a simple finite state machine, based on thresholds on the capacitive sensor values and their derivatives. The machine accepts sequences of the form 1-down-1-up-2-down-2-up, within a certain timeout. On reaching the final state, the gesture event is triggered.
Tap: User taps a finger on a single capacitive sensor.	The tap recogniser also uses a state machine, with state changes triggered by threshold crossings from a single capacitive sensor. When the capacitive sensor is quickly activated and deactivated, the appropriate event is generated.
Flick: User moves the device forwards, then backwards, in a quick, sharp motion, like cracking a whip.	Flicking is sensed by accelerometers. The flick recognizer uses a physical model of a point mass anchored via a spring inside a sphere with a simulated viscous fluid. Rapid motions overcome the attraction of the spring and the damping effect of the fluid to strike the wall of the sphere, triggering the gesture event.
Twist: The user turns the device through a 180 degree rotation.	Twisting is sensed by gyroscopes, using a leaky integrator which operates on a single angular axis. The gesture event is triggered when the integrator output crosses a threshold.

Four different gestures are recognised: stroke, tap, flick and twist (Table 1). These were selected as gestures that could easily be distinguished from each other, and which required little learning from users (based on results of informal pilot tests). Recognition of gestures is effected by an ensemble of simple models which are continuously and simultaneously run. These models combine elementary dynamical systems with finite state machines to recognise the movements.

These gestures are associated with audio-tactile messages, e.g. tapping on the device might result in the sound and sensation of tapping or hitting something, whereas twisting the device might result in the sound and feel of wine pouring or a key turning in a lock (additional mappings are presented in Section 4.3). Users can perform a single gesture to generate a short audio-tactile message or sequences of gestures to create a longer message containing multiple audio-tactile messages.

The SHAKE device features a three-way button, and the gesture recognition will only occur when this button is pressed, to avoid accidental triggering of gestures. This three-way button also determines the particular sound and vibration that will be produced, with three possible audio-tactile messages for each gesture (one for each of the up, middle and down positions). This limits the number of sounds per gesture to three; to access a wider palette of sounds, different themes could be created and the user could switch theme to access another sound set.

4.3 Shake2Talk Messages

Once the decision had been made to use audio-tactile messages for output and gesture interaction for input, the types of messages that people might wish to send were considered. It was discussed above that what is needed is a system that allows people to communicate in new expressive ways that are not too literal and which are open to interpretation by the sender and recipient. Therefore, the aim with this design was to create a set of audio-tactile messages but not to impose meanings. Instead, users could appropriate the messages for any function they wished, based on their own interpretation of the sounds. However, in order to select sounds it was beneficial to consider the scenarios in which people might wish to use this system. A brainstorming session was held to generate ideas about the types of scenarios in which the system might be used, and the types of sounds that people might want to send. The current uses of SMS and MMS along with the categories of touch in social communication were used to generate these ideas. In addition, the types of gestures which could be recognized were used as an inspiration, by considering what types of sounds might map to these gestures. Table 2 shows a list of possible scenarios along with the related sounds and gestures. The sounds are short, and synchronized with vibrotactile feedback. The vibrotactile sensations are designed to match the temporal pattern and amplitude contour of the sounds. For example the sound of tapping on wood is accompanied by gentle, short vibrotactile pulses, whereas the sound of hitting metal uses stonger, longer pulses. The sound of a cat purring is accompanied by a series of vibrotactile pulses that match the amplitude contour of the sound, and the resulting sensation feels much like that experienced when stroking a cat. To illustrate the system in use, three scenarios are described below.

Scenario 1: "Call when you can". Lucy wants to chat with her husband but it is not urgent, so she wants to indicate that he should call her when he has time. She picks up her *Shake2Talk* phone and taps on the device twice with her index finger. She hears and feels a gentle tapping, then presses send. When the message arrives on her husband's phone, his phone reproduces the same audio-tactile message, making a tapping sound and vibrating with a "tap" sensation. This analogy to someone tapping him on the shoulder indicates that he should contact her when he has a chance. In contrast, if the message were urgent, she might select a different output, such as tapping on a wine glass to indicate that a more urgent reply was needed.

Scenario 2: "Home safely". Bob leaves his parent's house for a long drive home. When he arrives home he picks up his *Shake2Talk* phone and makes a twist gesture, like turning a key in a lock. This sends an audio-tactile message with the sound and feel of a key turning in a lock to his mother. When it arrives on her phone she will hear and feel the message, and immediately know that Bob has arrived home safely. An SMS saying "home safely" would have required her to pick up the phone to look at the message: an audio-tactile message, on the other hand, is heard peripherally thus notifying her immediately even if she is engaged in another task.

Scenario 3: "I'm nervous". Mary is feeling nervous before an exam. By stroking her *Shake2Talk* phone, a heartbeat sound is generated. Mary strokes the device faster to speed up the heartbeat and then sends the message to her friend, Barbara. Barbara receives the sound and sensation of a heartbeat and is aware that Mary is nervous. She twists her phone to generate the sound of a glass of wine being poured and sends this back to Mary to indicate that she should relax and not worry.

Table 2. Possible scenarios, with corresponding sounds and gestures

Scenario	Sound	Gesture
"Call when you can"	Gentle tapping	Tap
"I need to talk to you"	Tapping on a wine glass	Tap
"Call me now (angry)"	Banging on metal	Tap
"Fancy a drink?"	Beer pouring	Twist
"Relax!"	Wine pouring	Twist
"Home Safely"	Key in lock	Twist
"Thinking of you"	Regular heartbeat	Stroke (regular speed)
"I'm nervous"	Racing heartbeat	Stroke (fast)
"I'm bored"	Snore	Stroke
"happy"	Cat purring	Stroke
"I'm rushing"	Fast footsteps	Twist back and forth
"I've put the dinner on"	Rattling of pots and pans	Twist back and forth
"Angry"	Plates smashing	Flick
"Playful slap"	Slap	Flick
"Hurry Up"	Whip crack	Flick

4.4 Evaluation

The next stage of this work is to deploy the *Shake2Talk* system with users to evaluate how it might be used for communication. In the first instance, the system will be deployed with four pairs of users (couples or close family members), over a four week period, and the use of the system will be monitored through data logging, interviews, and diaries to see how people use the system. In addition to recording their use of the system (and reflecting upon the data logged by the system), users will be asked to record their use of other communication methods during this period. During the four weeks users will try the system with the gesture interaction input method for two weeks and the menu selection input method for two weeks (the order will be counterbalanced between pairs), to investigate how the methods compare. A number of research questions will be addressed by this study:

1. When and where do people send audio-tactile messages? What kinds of messages do they send? What kinds of messages would they like to send (that are not currently available in the system)?
2. How is *Shake2Talk* used in combination with other forms of communication?
3. How does the use, and perception, of *Shake2Talk* differ when messages are created through gestures rather than menu selection?
4. Does the gift giving element of text messaging transfer to audio-tactile messaging? Is this dependent on the sender creating messages themselves?
5. What are the implications of the fact that the sound always announces itself upon arrival? Does this cause annoyance or raise privacy concerns?

This evaluation will provide insights into how people might use an audio-tactile messaging system alongside other communication methods. In addition, it will act as a probe to understand more about how people currently communicate, by prompting them to think about the kinds of messages they currently send, and how these could be replaced by audio-tactile communication. The system will then be refined and a longer term study will be conducted, so as to gain greater insights into long-term use.

5 Conclusions and Future Work

This paper has introduced *Shake2Talk*: a mobile communication system in which users create audio-tactile messages through simple gesture interactions with a mobile phone and send these to other *Shake2Talk* users. The aim of this research was to design a new form of messaging, using non-visual modalities. Audio and tactile modalities have been combined in these messages so as to benefit from the affordances of each. Vibrotactile messages are attention grabbing and will be felt even in noisy environments when an audio message might be missed. Combining these with audio messages means that a richer set of messages can be used, and less training is needed as people can use their real world associations with these sounds.

The problem with many new communication systems is that they are short lived, having novelty value with first use, but failing to be adopted in the long term. To succeed it has been suggested that a communication system needs to offer rich expression and allow users to interpret messages in their own way, rather than being limited to literal communication. *Shake2Talk* has been designed to allow people to express themselves in new ways, without imposing meanings on the types of messages that people can send, but only by long term deployment will we understand whether this has been achieved. Therefore, the *Shake2Talk* system will now be deployed with a number of users in a longitudinal evaluation. This evaluation will investigate how, when and why people use audio-tactile messaging to communicate, and will provide insight into how such a system might be adopted and used.

Acknowledgments. Thanks to the SDS Group at MSRC (in particular Abigail Sellen, Richard Harper and Phil Gosset) and to Dominic Robson for his work on the sound design. This research was conducted while John Williamson was an intern at MSRC.

References

1. Harper, R.: Towards a new Communications Genre. IEEE Computer On-Line Magazine, 99–101 (2005)
2. Harper, R., Hodges, S.: Beyond talk, beyond sound: Emotional expression and the future of mobile connectivity. In: Höflich, J., Hartmann, M. (eds.) Mobile Communication in Everyday Life: An Ethnographic View, Frank & Timme (2006)
3. Kasesniemi, E., Rautiainen, P.: Mobile Culture of Children and Teenagers in Finland. In: Katz, J.E., Aakhus, M.A. (eds.) Perpetual Contact: Mobile Communication, Private Talk, Public Performance, pp. 170–192. Cambridge University Press, Cambridge (2002)
4. Kopomaa, T.: The breakthrough of text messaging in Finland. In: Harper, R., Palen, L., Taylor, A. (eds.) The Inside Text: Social, Cultural and Design Perspectives on SMS, Springer, Heidelberg (2005)
5. Ling, R., Julsrud, T., Yttri, B.: Nascent communication genres within SMS and MMS. In: Harper, R., Palen, L., Taylor, A. (eds.) The Inside Text: Social, Cultural and Design Perspectives on SMS, Springer, Heidelberg (2005)
6. Taylor, A., Harper, R.: Age-old Practises in the 'New World': A study of gift-giving between teenage mobile phone users. In: Proc. CHI 2002, pp. 439–446. ACM Press, New York (2002)
7. Kindberg, T., Spasojevic, M., Fleck, R.: I saw this and thought of you: Some social uses of camera phones. In: Proc. CHI 2005, pp. 1545–1548. ACM Press, New York (2005)
8. Thayer, S.: Social Touching. In: Schiff, W., Foulke, E. (eds.) Tactual Perception: A Sourcebook, Cambridge University Press, Cambridge (1982)
9. Jones, S.E., Yarborough, E.: A Naturalistic Study of The Meanings of Touch. Communication Monographs 52(1), 19–56 (1985)
10. Haans, A., IJsselsteijn, W.: Mediated social touch: a review of current research and future directions. Virtual Reality 9(2), 149–159 (2006)
11. DiSalvo, C., et al.: The Hug: An Exploration of Robotic Form For Intimate Communication. In: ROMAN 2003, pp. 403–408. IEEE, Los Alamitos (2003)
12. Chang, A., et al.: ComTouch: Design of a Vibrotactile Communication Device. In: Proc. DIS 2002, pp. 312–320. ACM press, New York (2002)
13. Rovers, A.F., van Essen, H.A.: HIM: A Framework for Haptic Instant Messaging. In: Ext. Abstracts CHI 2004, pp. 1313–1316. ACM Press, New York (2004)
14. Smith, J., MacLean, K.E.: Communicating Emotion Through a Haptic Link: Design Space and Methodology. International Journal of Human-Computer Studies (IJHCS), Special Issue on Affective Evaluation–Innovative Approaches 65(4), 376–387 (2007)
15. Brown, L.M., Brewster, S.A., Purchase, H.C.: A First Investigation into the Effectiveness of Tactons. In: Proc. World Haptics 2005, pp. 167–176. IEEE, Los Alamitos (2005)
16. Chan, A., MacLean, K., McGrenere, J.: Learning and Identifying Haptic Icons under Workload. In: Proc. World Haptics 2005, pp. 432–439. IEEE, Los Alamitos (2005)
17. Brewster, S.A., Wright, P.C., Edwards, A.D.N.: A detailed investigation into the effectiveness of earcons. In: Proc. ICAD 1992, pp. 471–498. Addison-Wesley, Reading (1992)
18. Gaver, W.W.: The SonicFinder: An Interface that Uses Auditory Icons. Human Computer Interaction 4(1) (1989)
19. Gaver, W.W.: Sound Support For Collaboration. In: Proc. ECSCW 1991, pp. 293–308. Kluwer Academic Publishers, Dordrecht (1991)
20. Isaacs, E., Walendowski, A., Ranganathan, D.: Hubbub: A sound-enhanced mobile instant messenger that supports awareness and opportunistic interactions. In: Proc. CHI 2002, pp. 179–186. ACM Press, New York (2002)

Communication-Wear:
User Feedback as Part of a Co-Design Process

Sharon Baurley[1], Philippa Brock[1], Erik Geelhoed[2], and Andrew Moore[1]

[1] Central Saint Martins College of Art & Design, Southampton Row, London,
WC1B 4AP, UK
s.baurley@csm.arts.ac.uk, p.brock@csm.arts.ac.uk,
mail@andrewjmoore.co.uk
[2] Hewlett-Packard Labs, Building 3, Mail Stop 67, Filton Road, Stoke Gifford, Bristol,
BS34 8QZ, UK
erik_geelhoed@hp.com

Abstract. *Communication-Wear* is a clothing concept that augments the mobile phone by enabling expressive messages to be exchanged remotely, by conveying a sense of touch, and presence. It proposes to synthesise conventions and cultures of fashion with those of mobile communications, where there are shared attributes in terms of communication and expression. Using garment prototypes as research probes as part of an on-going iterative co-design process, we endeavoured to mobilise participants' tacit knowledge in order to gauge user perceptions on touch communication in a lab-based trial. The aim of this study was to determine whether established sensory associations people have with the tactile qualities of textiles could be used as signs and metaphors for experiences, moods, social interactions and gestures, related to interpersonal touch. The findings are used to inspire new design ideas for textile actuators for use in touch communication in successive iterations.

Keywords: Smart textiles, wearable technology, touch communication, clothing and emotion, user research, prototype as probe.

1 Introduction

With the downscaling of traditional textile industry in the EU, it is envisaged that, in Europe, a high-tech clothing sector will soon emerge [1]. First applications have already surfaced in the area of sports and health [2]. Looking further out into the future, it may only be a matter of time before some of these wearable and smart textile technologies are adopted within the fashion industry. However, as yet it is unclear what kind of compelling applications might accelerate the uptake of smart materials in the consumer market [3]. Fashion is uniquely placed as a future mediator of technology, in particular within the relatively new "experience economy"; a culture where the human senses, experiences, and emotions are more and more of commercial interest. The *Communication-Wear* concept seeks to operate within, and contribute to, the emergence of a new genre in clothing and fashion, where fashion and ICT converge. This research is multi-disciplinary, drawing on expertise from fashion and textile design, electronics, wearable computing, and user research.

I. Oakley and S. Brewster (Eds.): HAID 2007, LNCS 4813, pp. 56–68, 2007.

Communication-Wear proposes to marry conventions and cultures of fashion, as being an expressive medium that connects people with the social world, with principles of nonverbal communication and current cultures of mobile communications. Fashion/clothing and mediated communication technologies share common attributes in terms of how they enable people to construct an identity, to be expressive, to differentiate themselves, and which enables communication between people allowing them to form communities. People do this through their consumption of these commodities and services. The links between expression and nonverbal communication through body movement and touch in human communication have long been identified [4, 5, 6]. Mobile phones are already *'affective technologies – that is, objects which mediate the expression and exchange of feelings and emotions'* [7]. The design framework for *Communication-Wear* [8] is informed by these diverse strands of research.

Our research locates potential youth consumers at the centre of the development of fashion/clothing prototypes by engaging them as co-developers and evaluators. Using design-led techniques we aim to determine what and how people might communicate through augmented clothing, and how this might fit in with, and support their everyday communications. We developed a smart textile system and integrated it into prototype garments that provide a *menu* of touch expressions encompassing 'hug' and 'stroke' touch gestures that the garment can sense and actuate. In a way we used the prototypes as research probes as a means to create conditions in which participants could experience, play and dream, possibly gauging a deeper level of knowledge or tacit knowledge about user's desires, preferences and behaviours, as well as the way the concept makes them feel. Our approach aims to gain insight into what some of the catalysts and drivers of future consumer fashion wearable technology that permits touch communication might be, and to explore methods to design appropriable *smart* clothing. In order to do this we have conducted a series of studies using these probes to gain insight into how people might appropriate the functionality and create their own meanings through visual, aesthetic, and/or tactile codes. The immediate aim of the studies was to determine whether established sensory associations people have with the tactile qualities of textiles could be used as signs and metaphors for experiences, moods, social interactions and gestures, related to interpersonal touch. This is the third in a series of user studies, which forms an integral part of an iterative design process.

2 Related Work

There is no shortage of technology explorations in this area. Work in the area of remote communication through touch includes 'ComTouch' [9], a vibrotactile communication device, which augments remote voice communication with touch. The 'Lumitouch' [10] system consists of a pair of interactive picture frames. 'InTouch' [11] is an internet-based concept that aims to create the illusion that two people, separated by distance, are interacting with a shared physical object. *CuteCircuit* is developing its 'F+R Hugs' [12] into a commercial offering. 'TapTap' [13] is a wearable haptic system that allows human touch to be recorded, broadcast and played back for emotional therapy. Our approach differs in the sense that we have elicited and systematically analysed user feedback with the view to inform or inspire designers of fashion from a social science angle.

3 *Communication-Wear* Design Framework

We have taken a design-led approach in this research, as we are proposing artefacts for consumption. Design is at the interface between technology or material and the consumer. As we are dealing specifically with wearable technology, fashion and textile design methods play a key role in our process.

The point of departure for most studies of dress and fashion is consumer culture, a cultural system of making meaning, and of making meaning through what we consume. Consumer culture is, what Raymond Williams [14] has called, the *"bricks and mortar of everyday life"*, the music you listen to, the clothes you wear, etc. These are all aspects of material culture, which most studies of fashion draw on to look at the way we use it to map out identities for ourselves. *"Fashion, clothing and dress constitute signifying systems in which a social order is constructed and communicated"*. [15] Meanings can be generated as a result of negotiations between people resulting from their joint actions, e.g., communication as social interaction through messages [16], which constitutes an individual as a member of a group. In the Semiotic (or Structuralist) model of communication as identified by Fisk, *"it is the process of communication that produces or generates meanings"* [15], in which both sender and receiver are constituted. The designer can be the source of the meaning of the garment, *"a product of the designer's intentions, where intentions are defined as a person's thoughts, feelings, beliefs desires about the world and the things in it"*. [15] Similarly, wearers can attribute their own meanings to the garment, thereby expressing their own beliefs, hopes and fears *"through their use of the garment"* [15].

Textiles have a range of tactile qualities, which textile and fashion designers have always exploited as part of their design method to engineer a look, concept, mood etc. There are well-established descriptors for the sensory associations and *hand* qualities of textiles used in the fashion and textile industry, e.g., smooth-rough, soft-crisp, cool-warm, delicate-coarse, hard-soft, etc. The descriptors along with other attributes, such as colour, shape, and pattern, are used by fashion designers as a legitimate design method to develop seasonal design collections. Depending upon how they are consumed, these collections can become a part of consumer culture.

In the same way that youth groups create new languages using SMS, so *smart* clothing will need a design palette or *language*, which users can co-opt, adapt and assign their own meanings to, or make their own meanings with. A range of textile actuation types such as shape-change, light-emitting, and tactility, has been designed during the course of this research. The aim of the user studies is to determine whether established sensory associations people have with the tactile qualities of textiles could be used as signs and metaphors for experiences, moods, social interactions and gestures related to interpersonal touch.

The team designed the garments and their textiles according to these sensory associations and design principles, as well as drawing upon their own experiences and associations. Designers often reference their own experiences. A fabric that has a warm handle is generally understood to have comforting associations; synonyms of warm include having or displaying warmth or affection, passionate and psychologically warm, friendly and responsive, caring, fond, tender. A designer devising a fashion collection will start with a concept board that communicates the mood on a visual and tactile level. If the collection has a *warm* mood, the designer will include in his/her concept board swatches of fabric that are warm to the touch, a warm colour palette, as well as images or photographs that communicate a sense of warm. In this prototype the author employed a heatable textile as a means to engender these feelings in a person when receiving touch messages.

4 Prototype Technology Platform

The initial stages of development of the technology platform of the prototype have been reported in a separate article [17]. In short, each garment is twinned with a mobile phone via Bluetooth. Communication between garments takes place as follows: Both the sender and the receiver (wearer of the garment) carry a mobile phone. A text message from the sender's mobile phone sends an instruction to the receiver's Bluetooth-enabled mobile phone. This then sends an instruction to the recipient's garment. Users can also send touch messages by gesturing them, as opposed to using text. Textile gesture (mechanical stretch) sensors were located on the upper back where the arm joins the trunk of the body, in order to capture self-hug actions, and touch sensors were situated on the lower parts of the sleeves [18]. Galvanic Skin Response (GSR) was integrated into the lining of the garment looping around the index and second finger on the left hand. Woven textile circuits carried power and data signals.

Actuation of *hug* touch messages took place via shape-shifting textiles combined with the generation of heat, symbolising the warming sensation felt when touched by another person. When a hug or embrace gesture is sent, the shape-shifting textile contracts and heat is generated. A tactile actuator that attempted to simulate someone touching or pulling on the wearer's sleeve was engineered using shape memory alloy wire. When an arm touch message is sent, the sleeve of the jacket moves up the arm. The placement of these actuators is informed by Argyle's 'vocabulary of touch' [19]. Light-emitting diodes were engineered into the garment on the cuffs of the sleeves. LEDs were fabricated onto a conductive textile tracks in the garment. This light-emitting section was linked to the GSR, so that when the skin conductivity of a wearer changes, this section lights up on the other wearer's jacket.

Thus, a participant by hugging themselves and stretching the mechanical stretch sensors was able to deliver a contracting/pulling and warming sensation to the upper back of the recipient. A touch on either of the arms by the sender was received as the sleeve moving up the arm. The recipient receives the touch message through actuation, as well as an SMS confirmation, saying 'hug shared', or 'left touch shared', etc. The SMS platform was developed by Vodafone, UK. In addition, physiological arousal, as detected by the GSR sensors, was relayed to the partner by light being emitted from the fibre-optic section. The GSR took the form of textile electrodes integrated into a semi-glove configuration at the end of the sleeve in the garment, which wrapped around the index and second finger. GSR can detect levels of arousal; it cannot detect emotion on its own. All electronic textiles used in this prototype were produced using a weaving process and silver-coated nylon yarn.

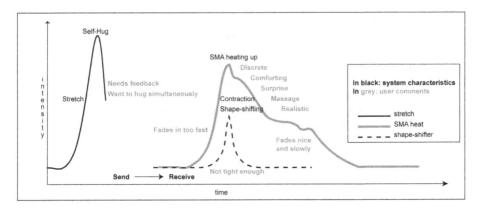

Fig. 1. Communication-Wear jacket

5 User Feedback

Four pairs of participants took part, a total of seven women and one man (aged between twenty and twenty-five), who were recruited locally. The participants were briefed on the functionality of the garments, which was also demonstrated to them. The participants then spent a period of time exchanging sensory messages or touch communication in the Watershed Media Centre, Bristol, UK. Afterwards pairs were interviewed together. Through having experienced the tactile sensation in relation to its given meaning, participants were asked to describe and articulate the particular qualities the sensation engendered, and compare those with their own experiences and associations. Participants were also asked to relate their experience with the prototype to their current mobile phone communication practices. All sessions were video-recorded and transcribed.

Fig. 2. Briefing participants

Fig. 3. Participants in the Watershed, Bristol

Sensations of Touch or Presence. In terms of describing how the heat/contraction felt, the majority of participants volunteered adjectives such as *"warm"*, *"comforting"*, *"nice"*, *"pleasant"*. *Comforting* seems to be how many participants understood or related to the warming sensation: *"I personally really like the heat only because that's naturally a very comforting and warm feeling."* A couple of the participants suggested that the hug actuator related to their associations of massage, which also has connotations of comfort: *"It feels like a little massage in a way."* *"When I sat with my arms like that and it was stroking across the back."*

In terms of whether the heat/contraction sensation was like a hug or touch to them, only two suggested it was: *"It was a little bit like a hug, a very light hug, someone just gently putting their hands on your back." "The sensation I felt was more the heat of it."* Even though the sensation of the shape-shifting textile didn't correlate with most participants' associations of a hug touch, many thought it was a nice sensation: *"It doesn't feel like a hug, but it's nice though, a nice sensation."*

A number of participants remarked on the importance of receiving almost instant feedback from sent touch messages, to 'hug' instantaneously: *"... it would have been nice if one person started off, and then the other person hugs back, and then you think, 'oh I've got a hug back'."*

A couple of participants suggested that the touch actuation is most effective when the recipient isn't expecting it: *"When I went to the bar to get a drink, she was sitting down and then I did it* (sent hug touch message) *whilst I was in the queue ... she exclaimed 'ooh, ooh, it was nice'."*

A number of participants volunteered comments on the frequency of the contraction of the shape-shifting textile actuator: *"I think the only thing was that it felt like a very fast action, I felt it may have worked better if it was slower."* It was also suggested that there should be some kind of spectrum to reflect the differences in how different people touch: *"There would be a huge difference between someone giving you a long slow squeeze and something quite jerky."*

When discussing the touch actuator located on the arm, the majority of participants said that it was too subtle to notice visually: *"If somebody was touching you you'd want to be able to feel the pressure."* Participants suggested that they were *"expecting to feel a stroke"*, or *"something rubbing against"* their skin, *"like grabbing onto your arm, pulling"*. Only one participant said that they gleaned some kind of touch sensation: *"I grabbed my arm and it did kind of feel that I was being touched a little bit, but I just felt like the movement wasn't necessarily* (distinct) *... but there was some communication there."* The touch actuator on the arm being *"more visible than being able to feel it"* presented some participants with social dilemmas: *"I think some of the movements were just too subtle, unless you were really staring, and then you look silly as everyone else in the bar is staring at you."*

The majority of participants thought that the hug actuator was *"the most effective one"*: *"I can kind of really see the point of the hug one, and it was very emotive and quite intimate and stuff, but the sleeve tugging one ... I think it's harder to see the point of sending it to somebody."* The majority of participants said that they would prefer to feel a touch message, rather than see it: *"I preferred the sensation, the visual thing didn't really mean anything to me, the feeling was nicer." "... that's more 'huggish' and more private."*

A number of participants liked the aesthetic of the light-emitting textiles: *"I like the way it glows through the fabric, so it's not just lights on the outside." "The sleeves lighting up was sort of a bit of a thrill."* But many felt quite conspicuous when they 'lit up' in public: *"I put them under the table for a while, especially when I was sitting on my own, it was a bit odd."* One or two participants didn't feel conspicuous, saying that the technology in the jackets was quite discrete, and that the meaning behind the light-emitting textiles could be a positive force in a public space: *"It's quite discreet, and I guess if a lot of people were aware of what it meant, that you sort of hugged or touched someone and they were feeling good about it, it might be like 'oh he feels good' or 'someone's just sent a good signal'".*

A few participants said that they liked the fact that the light-emitting textiles provided a mechanism to acknowledge their messages: *"I really like that you know they are receiving it, you know they're feeling that sensation." "... it looked quite nice as well, glowing, and gave you a nice warm feeling even though it's not warm."*

Another participant also liked the idea of personal display: *"I think the light is a good idea, if it indicated mood or something like that"*, whilst some participants wondered whether they would want to display their moods and emotions on their clothing: *"It's quite different from your own clothing reflecting a change in your mood, and your mood being reflected on somebody else."* Or, whether the ability to read mood through your clothing could be positive: *"In terms of trying to track your mood swings and whether there are patterns to your behaviour,* (and pairing) *that with other information, like where you were at that time ... is quite interesting."*

Other Tactile Actuation Types Engendering Touch or Presence. Inspired by the 'touch' sensations they experienced in the prototypes, we asked participants to try to project their associations of touch in terms of sensations or aspects of material culture. A number of participants volunteered types of sensations as well as other parts of the body where such actuation could be cited: *"A tickle would be quite good if you could send them a tickle." "Like a pinch." "If you had a sensor on the neck that would be a really interesting situation because your neck is so sensitive and also quite a central area." "Could you have like a vibration?"* One or two participants came up other gestures or actions that more closely correlated with touch for them: *"Sending a message to a friend like squeezing their hand sort of thing."*

Participants talked about assigning their own meaning or codes to different types of actuation depending upon the recipient, and their knowledge of that person. Aspects such as being able to *"change the wavelets"* of a *"stroke pattern"* to achieve *"different frequencies"* of *"a general touching sensation like a tapping"* were discussed: *"With sign language the same sign can be done in loads of different ways for different meanings."* One participant suggested that it is about *"suitable gestures ... because depending on who you are talking to, you will vary your* (approach); *so a hug with someone I haven't seen for ages would be a different hug with my fiancé."*

Many participants suggested that the garment should be *"set up for individual preferences"*, *"to change the given options with what in your case a hug means or a touch means"*: *"I think it's more important you receive the message and you feel it in a way that's personal and it actually feels like that intended signal ... that tingle down your arm ... meant something to you."*

Relating this Type of Communication to Mobile Communication Practices.
Many participants saw this type of touch communication being combined with mobile phone functions, e.g., interacting with the people they are talking to: *"When ... you're talking normally you could activate a hug mode."* Examples around text messaging included incorporating an icon into a text that symbolised a touch, which then triggered actuation: *"... it should be sent with a text message and then you put a symbol in so it would be a bit more intuitive, like a smiley."*

Participants' ideas were very creative around what they would use this communication for: *"I would send a hug to someone if they were kind of sad, and I'd probably send a nudge to someone if I wanted them to do something." "... thinking about multi-media messages and stuff you could include it* (hug) *in a photo to someone you haven't seen for a while, or a sound clip."*

One or two participants talked about using this communication with people who are in the vicinity, for example in public settings where they want to communicate privately: *"I sort of see it as communicating across the room, like at a dinner party, where you want to say 'hi' to your partner, but you can't really do anything because it's inappropriate, so you send them a hug or just a touch on the arm." "... you just want to remind someone you're there. It's very private."*

Other participants talked about this type of communication having a value over distance: *"... maybe I'm having a bad day and I just want to hug my fiancé, and he could send one back. ... someone's there for you."*

One participant in one pair asked whether touch communication *"would be any greater than if you got a text message?"*, to which the other participant replied: *"Yes, because the text message is taking too much time; it's that 'one-click' philosophy of simple mechanisms, where something that quick and easy can be a lot more effective."*

Many participants liked the subtle nature of the touch actuation, and the fact that they were communicating remotely with someone unbeknown to those in their vicinity: *"You can continue having a conversation with someone, and you've just got that warmth sensation, and you think 'oh someone thought about me' and that's just really, really nice. ... no-one else can participate, it's that kind of secret feeling."*

One participant lauded the use of language in the SMS platform, saying it was nice *"to have that record"*: *"It was really nice to say 'oh yes they got it', and 'shared' is a really nice word for it as well because it is kind of sharing."*

A couple of participants talked about the warmth of tactile communication, in contrast to email and text messaging: *"There's something about* (the fact that) *somebody has actually done something physical. I find email quite cold sometimes."*

Similar problems that occur with current technologies may, it was suggested by one participant, beleaguer touch communication: *"People get used to putting a kiss at the end of their text messages, and because everybody does it all the time it's lost its meaning, and that would probably happen with this over time."*

Participants were split in terms of with whom they would use this type of communication; some said everyone, some only family and friends in their trusted group, and some only partners, girl/boyfriends: *"I would use it with anyone I send a text message to, a friend or whatever, family." "My nephews and nieces ... it would be quite nice if I could send them a hug or everyone I miss."*

Table 1. Summary of main findings

Actuator	Likes	Dislikes	Communicate	User wishes	Adjectives
Heat Contraction (Back)	•Nice sensation •Subtle •Hug is most effective •Massage	•Mostly not like a hug •Putting hands on your back	Split: Conspicuous vs. inconspicuous in a public setting	•Instant feedback •Spectrum of touch intensities •Distinct & positive •Sensations: Tickle, pinch, vibration, pressure	•Warm •Comforting •Nice •Pleasant •Emotive •Intimate
Stroke (Upper arm)		-Too subtle -Visual has no meaning		•Expect to feel something rather than see it	
Light-emitting (Wrists/cuffs)	•Aesthetic •Thrill (meaning unknown to bystanders) •Emotional insight	•Conspicuous •Embarrassing	Split: Showing emotions or mood		•Glowing •Warm •Pretty
All			•'Warm' communication Split: •Everyone •Only family & friends (trusted) •Only partners	•Meaning-making •SMS touch icon •Touch with voice •Remote private communication in public •Across distance	

6 Discussion

In this trial we asked pairs of participants to don a fashionable denim jacket to exchange touch messages via mobile phones. In a previous laboratory-based experiment [20], a similar array of touch messaging was available which indicated that a hug had a deep emotional impact, fibre optics lighting up induced a sense of wonder, somehow the inner physiological and/or psychological life of the sender was reflected (literally) in the recipient's clothes, whereas the stroking gesture was received as a more playful, tickling action, rather than tenderness. A natural next design step was to try out *Communication-Wear* in a more realistic setting. Lab studies potentially have high construct validity, whereas field-trials help to fortify ecological validity. The Watershed Media Centre is a popular meeting place for the Bristol media world, students and artists.

Sending and receiving a hug elicited an abundance of comments in this study, most of them signifying a deeply emotional and private communication, not visually noticed by the other people in the bar. Figure 4 summarises the mechanism and user feedback of sending and receiving a hug. The X-axis shows the progression of time, whilst the Y-axis depicts a hypothesised intensity of feeling from both the sender's and the receiver's experience angle.

Fig. 4. Sending and receiving a hug

Crossing one's arms requires intensity, and we hypothesize that this act of self-hug is one of high emotional intensity. In the graph we depicted this as having a higher intensity than receiving a hug. In this study we have concentrated on the recipient of the hug. The receiver of a hug felt both a warming sensation and a contraction. Concluding from the number and type of comments, the heat was clearly experienced stronger than the contraction of the textile. This is reflected in the height (and width) of the graphs. The fading of the warmth at a relatively slower pace, compared to the onset of the heat and the rather quick contractions met with emotional appreciation. One design point therefore that needs attention is that of synchronising both the temporal and intensity aspects, such that the two curves, heat and shape shifting, are more in sync. In addition by concentrating on both qualitative and quantitative measurement in future studies, we might attempt to gauge and bring-in line the giving and receiving of a hug in terms of intensity and actuation over time. Volunteers also highlighted the half duplex nature of the hug communication as they wished to hug each other simultaneously.

The GSR-induced lighting up of the diodes in the cuffs of the jacket had a different effect on different people. Some found it rather conspicuous and embarrassing, whereas others enjoyed the thrill of pretty lights lighting up on their clothing, mapping-on well to the psycho-physiological activation from within the sender. Some also found this thrilling as the lights were thought to be discrete as bystanders would not be able to guess what triggered them. Inevitably the topic of mood-sensing came up, and although we are a long way off from being able to accurately assess peoples' moods, the lights were still experienced as something magical. Given the opportunity people judge relatively, but their first experience of their first actuator is judged in absolute terms, or rather they will compare it to something from a non-actuator world. From the video footage those first experiences are the most surprising, exhilarating ones. If they experience a hug first and then the jacket arm movement, then the second one is not experienced as intensively as the first.

Based upon our findings, it is possible that the tactile sensations generated by electronic or smart textiles can stand for metaphors or signs for touch, gesture and expression. Participants' experience of the warming textiles elicited many comments around 'comfort'. One or two participants suggested that the act of doing something physical was special, compared to email communication, which they found to be cold, thus suggesting that this physical communication is the antonym, warm. Those who couldn't associate the warm contracting textile with a hug, suggested it felt like being touched. A small number of participants responded positively to the light-emitting textiles, using the adjective 'glowing', to describe both the radiance, and the feeling of warmth these textiles elicited. The actuator on the arm was largely misunderstood as it was meant to signify someone trying to gain the attention of the wearer. However, it produced interesting comments about the representation of touch being a distinct sensation that is discrete, rather than a public display.

This has been an iterative process: First concept testing (first study), then a lab experiment (2nd study), and then taking it out into a real world (but controlled) environment, always with the aim to gauge how this translates into an actual desire to wear such a system. With every step we know more; participants were keenly aware that only once a concept such as this reaches tipping point, will we see emergent consumer behaviour and the generation of 'smart' material culture, whose meanings are widely accepted and understood. For example, a number of participants related touch communication to the use of *smileys* in SMS. With reference to fashion theory discourse, some participants' views accorded with the meanings assigned to some touch actuations by the author, whilst a greater number of participants volunteered ways in which they might devise their own meanings as a result of social interaction through messages. This reflects what is happening in both mobile and web-based communications, and one participant related the development of language in these media to *Communication-Wear*.

This current study adds empirical user data, which are currently still rare. We have been pleasantly surprised and encouraged by how personal and emotional the responses have been to our haptic interventions thus far.

7 Conclusion

The findings from this study should be taken as a start to try to gain insights and understandings around this kind of communication using consumer fashion wearable technology. We adopted an experimental design approach in that we're using prototypes as research *probes,* and using the language of our material culture, namely fashion and textiles, as the focus for this research. We used a relatively small test sample, because we wanted to carry out an in-depth exploration, rather than general perceptions from a larger body. We have started to explore people's sensory associations of touch, and to relate those to textile attributes in order to gain inspiration for new designs for the actuation of touch communication. We have also generated data that suggests how people might use this kind of touch communication to support or complement their current communication practices.

Acknowledgments. This research is supported by the Arts and Humanities Research Council through the AHRC's Fellowships in the Creative and Performing Arts scheme, UK.

References

1. Euratex, European Technology Platform for the Future of Textiles and Clothing, (2004)
2. Paradiso, R., Loriga, G., Taccini, N.: Wearable Health-Care System for Vital Signs Monitoring. IFMBE Proceedings of Health Telematics, vol. 6 (2004)
3. Photopoulos, S.: Smart Fabrics and Interactive Textiles. VDC (June 2006)
4. Ekman, P., Friesen, W.: The Repertoire of Non-Verbal Behaviour: Categories, Origins, Usage, and Coding, Semiotica 1 (1969)
5. Jones, S.E., Yarborough, A.E.: A Naturalistic Study of the Meanings of Touch. Communication Monographs, 52 (1985)
6. Morris, C.: People Watching. Vintage, London (2002)
7. Lasen, A., Comparative, A.: Study of Mobile Phone Use in Public Spaces in London, Madrid and Paris, Vodafone (2002)
8. Baurley, S.: Interaction Design in Smart Textiles Clothing and Applications. In: Tao, X. (ed.) Wearable Electronics and Photonics, Woodhead, Cambridge (2005)
9. Chang, A., O'Modhrain, S., Jacob, R., Gunther, E., Ishii, H.: ComTouch: Design of a Vibrotactile Communication Device. In: Proceedings of Designing Interactive Systems (2002)
10. Chang, A., Koerner, B., Resner, B., Wang, X.: An Emotional Communication Device. In: Extended abstracts of Conf. on Human Factors in Computing Systems, pp. 313–314. ACM Press, New York (2002)
11. Brave, S., Dahley, A.: A Medium for Haptic Interpersonal Communication. In: Conf. on Human Factors in Computing Systems (1997)
12. www.cutecircuit.com/now/projects/wearables/fr-hugs
13. Bonanni, L., Lieberman, J., Vaucelle, C., Zuckerman, O.: TapTap: A Haptic Wearable for Asynchronous Distributed Touch Therapy. In: Proceedings of Human-Computer Interaction (2006)
14. Williams, R.: Culture, Fontana New Sociology Series. Glasgow, Collins (1981)
15. Barnard, M.: Fashion as Communication, Routledge, London (1996)

16. Fiske, J., O'Sullivan, T.: Key Concepts in Communication and Cultural Studies. Routledge, London (1994)
17. Randell, C., Baurley, S., Chalmers, M., Müller, H.: Textile Tools for Wearable Computing. In: Proceedings of the 1st International Forum on Applied Wearable Computing (2004)
18. Randell, C., Baurley, S., Anderson, I., Müller, H., Brock, P.: The Sensor Sleeve: Sensing Affective Gestures. In: Workshop Proceedings of 9th IEEE International Symposium on Wearable Computers., IEEE Computer Society Press, Los Alamitos (2005)
19. Argyle, M.: Bodily Communication. Routledge, London (2001)
20. Baurley, S., Geelhoed, E.: Communication-Wear: User Feedback as Part of a Co-Design Process. In: Proceedings of The Good, The Bad And The Unexpected (2007)

Interactive Racing Game
with Graphic and Haptic Feedback

Sang-Youn Kim[1] and Kyu-Young Kim[2]

[1] IVR Lab., Korea University of Technology and Education, 307 Gajeonri,
Byeongcheon-myeon, Cheonan-si, 330-708, Chungnam, Korea
sykim@kut.ac.kr
[2] Samsung Advanced Institute of Technology(SAIT), Mt, 14-1, Nongseo-dong, Gigeung-gu,
Youngin-si, 449-712, Gyunggi-do, Korea
ncls@samsung.com

Abstract. This paper proposes a mobile racing game prototype system where a player haptically senses the state of a car and the road condition with a vibrotactile signal generation method. The vibrotactile signal generation method provides variable vibrotactile effects according to a user's interaction with the graphic environment. The generated vibrotactile effects are used for the input of an eccentric vibration motor and a solenoid actuator in order to convey vibrotactile information with a large bandwidth to the players. To evaluate the proposed racing game, six persons experience two kinds of racing game; one with vibrotactile feedback, the other without vibrotactile feedback. The experiment shows that the proposed game with vibrotactile feedback provides players with increased levels of realism and immersion.

Keywords: Vibrotactile, Haptic, Racing game.

1 Introduction

The game industry is currently experiencing rapid growth. As computer graphics, multi-media, and 3D sound technologies are increasingly incorporated into games, game development is rapidly becoming a core industry. In particular, in the near future mobile games are expected to show the fastest growth rates. According to industry analysts *Frost & Sullivan*, the global mobile game industry, which generated 436.4 million US dollars in 2002, will balloon to 9.34 billion dollars by 2008. Generally, mobile game developers have focused on the generation of 3D graphic environments and the stereo sound. However, it is not easy to provide immersive or realistic experiences to game players because the visual display units are small and insufficient to provide engrossing sensations to the players.

Users can communicate and/or interact with their mobile devices efficiently using haptic feedback. However, most haptic actuators that directly provide force or distributed pressure are too bulky to fit into mobile devices. Therefore, for mobile devices, haptic researchers have focused on stimulating the skin of users. There are four major mechanoreceptors [2] (Meissner corpuscle, Merkel's disk, Ruffini ending, and Pacinian corpuscle) in the human glabrous skin. Merkel's disks respond

I. Oakley and S. Brewster (Eds.): HAID 2007, LNCS 4813, pp. 69–77, 2007.

to quasi-static deformations of the skin, such as force or displacement in the frequency range of 0.4 Hz to 3 Hz [2]. They play an important role in detecting spatial structures in static contact, such as an edge or a bar. Ruffini endings react to buzz-like sensations in the frequency range of 100-500 Hz [2]. Meissner corpuscles, which have a frequency range of 2 Hz to 40 Hz, detect dynamic deformations of the skin such as the sensation of flutter [2]. Pacinian corpuscles, which have a frequency response in the range of 40 Hz to 500 Hz, are the most sensitive to vibration amplitude and are particularly known to serve as the detector of accelerations and vibrations [2].

A vibrotactile signal is a practical way to stimulate human skin in mobile devices. Indeed, vibrotactile motors already appear in many commercial mobile devices,most notably mobile phones. There has also been useful research conducted on vibrotactile feedback in mobile devices. B.L.Harrison et al. [3] describe a tactile user interface for controlling mobile devices. T.Kaaresoja and J.Linjama [4] determined that the duration of a control signal for generating vibration should be between 50 and 200 milliseconds. A.Chang et al. [5] developed a mobile device for providing vibrotactile information coupled with auditory information called ComTouch. This system allowed rich communication between users by converting hand pressure into vibration intensity. J.Lindjama et al. [6] proposed a gesture interface for mobile devices equipped with an accelerometer and a vibration motor. In their research, they discussed specific features of a haptic interaction method for mobile devices and constructed a sensor-based movement detection system with haptic feedback. I.Oakley et al. [7],[8] developed a hardware platform with motion sensing input and vibrotactile output and applied the platform to the specific scenario of scrolling. Y.Sekiguchi et al. [9] developed a new type of a haptic interface which enables users to feel haptic sensations as if a mobile device has a small object inside it when they shake the mobile device. I.Poupyrev et al. [10] developed a low power tactile actuator (the TouchEngine), which can produce a wide variety of tactile sensations for mobile devices. Finally, Immersion Corporation [11] has developed the VibTonz® system for increasing the quality the messages that can be sent via vibration.

Many mobile devices currently have a commercially available eccentric motor with an operating frequency of between 100 Hz to 250 Hz. The eccentric motor generates concentrated force which is proportional to the square of the number of the motor's revolutions. Hence, the vibrotactile effect obtained from an eccentric motor is suitable for representing alert signals. However, it is not easy to generate a set of vibrotactile stimuli that are easily discriminated from one another as humans are relatively insensitive to differences in vibration frequency in the high frequency range (above 100Hz). Conversely, the resolution of human frequency perception is greater in the low frequency range (below 100Hz). That means that human operators can easily discriminate 1Hz vibrotactile stimuli from 2Hz stimuli, and 2Hz from 4Hz. However, it is extremely hard for them to discriminate between vibrotactile stimuli at 200Hz and 250Hz. Due to this lack of sensitivity in the high frequency region, the use of an eccentric motor limits our ability to discriminate diverse vibrotactile sensations. Consequently, in order to provide a range of sensations to users, it is necessary to consider an actuator which can generate vibrotactile information with a large bandwidth. In this paper, we combine an eccentric motor and a solenoid actuator for creating a concentrated force and a variety of vibrotactile sensations.

Even by selecting an actuator configuration with a large bandwidth, the lack of sophisticated methods for vibrotactile signal generation means that it is challenging to provide realistic tactile sensations to users as they touch or manipulate a real object. This paper incorporates a vibrotactile signal generation method [12] that provides game players with haptic sensations according to their interactions and presents a racing game prototype system where the generation method is used to enable players to sense a wide variety of vibrotactile patterns according to the velocity of a car and the roughness of the displayed graphical environment.

2 Haptic Effect in Racing Game

In conventional interaction systems like games, vibrotactile effects have been used to represent simple events (for example, the collision between two objects) to players. In this section, we introduce a vibrotactile signal generation method [12] which can provide haptic sensation according to variable game states (for example, the velocity of a car, a normal/abnormal track, a bump on a road, and so on).

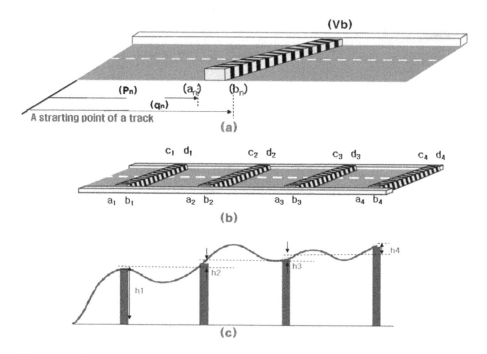

Fig. 1. A racing track and virtual blocks (a): a racing track containing a virtual block, (b) : virtual blocks on a racing track, and (c) : height of a racing track

For generating a variety of vibrotactile sensations, we introduced the concept of a virtual block [12]. Figure 1(a) shows a racing track containing a virtual block. We selected two points (a_n and b_n) along the racing track and constructed a small potion (Vb) based on these two points on the racing track. This portion can consist of a single polygon or two or more polygons. In [12], we defined this portion to be a virtual block. The virtual block can be placed on a portion of the track where two discrete track units meet as shown in Figure 1(b). The unit track is the basic element for composing the racing track, as a polygon is a basic element for constructing an object. The unit track can consist of one or more polygons. The virtual blocks are not graphically displayed because they are insubstantial objects whose only purpose is to allow the model based generation of vibrations.

In our game system, the racing track has coordinate values in 3D space. Figure 1(c) shows the side view of the 3D racing track. In Figure 1(b), long bars show the virtual blocks and small circles in Figure 1(c) show the portions where the virtual blocks exist. The basic idea of proposed vibrotactile signal generation method is to generate a control input for vibrotactile signal when a player's car passes over a virtual block. The frequency of the control input for the vibrotactile effects therefore depends not only on the gap between the virtual blocks but also the car's velocity. In order to compute the frequency, we define the distance between the starting point of a track and the starting point of n-th virtual block as p_n, and the distance between the starting point of the track and the ending point of n-th virtual block as q_n. The amplitude of the control input is proportional to a difference (h_n) between the height of the current unit track and that of the previous unit track. The control input signal (V_T) for vibrotactile effects can be calculated by equation (1).

$$V_T(L) = \sum_{n=1} h_n [u(L - p_n) - u(L - q_n)] \tag{1}$$

Where,
u : a unit step function, and
L : the distance from starting point to the current position of a car

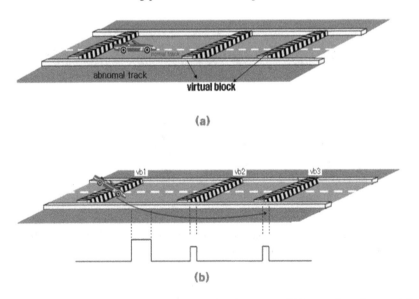

(a)

(b)

Fig. 2. Vibrotactile rendering in abnormal track (a): a normal/abnormal track containing a virtual block, (b): pulse input in abnormal track

The virtual block can be extended to form an abnormal track which generates vibrotactile sensations when a player's car is driven on flat ground (Figure 2). To achieve this, the virtual block is laid on an area where a normal track meets with an abnormal track (Figure 3). Due to this extended virtual block, we can haptically simulate the situation when a player's car is driven from a normal track to an abnormal track and for the duration that they drive along the abnormal track. For more information, refer to our previous research [12].

3 Racing Game

The proposed racing game system consists of two parts: a track editor and a racing game). Needless to say, tracks are designed in the editor, and then played in the game. These two systems are described in the following sections.

3.1 A Track Editor

In the developed game, a car can accelerate, decelerate, or change its direction on a 3D racing track according to the player's commands. A track editor was developed to design the racing tracks (Figure 3).

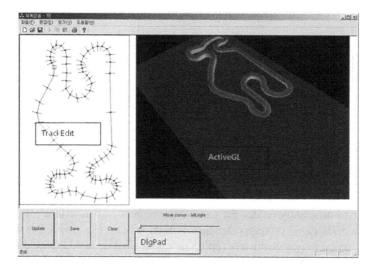

Fig. 3. Track Editor

The track editor consists of three parts: TrackEdit, ActiveGL, and DlgPad. Through TrackEdit, users can create or modify the shape of the racing track. To produce the racing track, a user makes unit tracks using the mouse buttons. They can also drag and rotate the unit tracks around the race course to rearrange it. After that, the user can create a smooth track by combining the individual unit tracks using TrackEdit. The ActiveGL part plays a role in constructing the 3D structure of the racing track by extracting height information from the unit tracks. The DlgPad consisting of three buttons and one slider and saves and updates the 3D racing track. These three buttons serve to transmit the user's command to the track environment.

- Update button: converts a 2D track to 3D using height information.
- Save button: saves the track.
- Clear button: initializes the track.
- Slider: adjusts the height information of the track.

3.2 Game Software Architecture

We implemented a multimodal racing game prototype where a player can experience visual and haptic information in order to increase immersion or realism. All parts except for the graphic rendering were realized in a mobile phone. The graphic programming was implemented on a PC platform using VC++ and Microsoft's DirectX API. Serial communication (RS232C) was used for data communication between the PC and mobile phone.

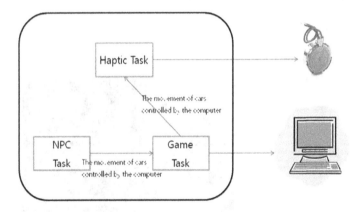

Fig. 4. The software architecture of the proposed game

In order to efficiently render the game environment and state to a player in real-time, our mobile game prototype features a multi-tasking framework consisting of a game task, a non-player characters (NPC) task, and a haptic task. Figure 4 shows this software architecture. The NPC task computes the movement of cars (except the car controlled by the user) and passes this data to the game task. The game task computes the velocity and the position of the player's car (the car controlled by the game player). The game task also checks for collisions between the player's car and obstacles such as other cars or the edges of the track, and renders the game environment. Furthermore, the game task passes the velocity of the player's car and the road condition to the haptic task in order to generate the vibrotactile stimuli. The haptic task controls the haptic actuators according to the amount of player's interaction with the game environment to provide haptic sensations to the player.

3.3 Graphic Feedback

Visual information constitutes more than 80% of the information perceived by a human's five senses; the human eye is a highly developed organ and its actions are well documented. The recent evolution of embedded technology has made it possible for the development of the 3D games on mobile devices. 3D mobile games can provide considerable immersion and excitement for their players. Hence, the proposed game was developed in a 3D environment in order to provide realistic visual information to players. The car controlled by the player is driven on a track as determined by the player's input on the phone keypad. Figure 5 shows the game environment.

Fig. 5. The proposed game environment

3.4 Haptic Feedback

Most mobile games display graphics and audio information to players and sometimes convey a vibration signal to alert users to a critical event (for example, collision with an object). To enhance the realism in the mobile games, haptic information should be complimentarily combined with visual and sound information and presented to players as a cohesive whole. In the case of mobile games, since the LCD size is limited, the haptic information may be a more important factor than visual information in increasing immersion. In this paper, we described an immersive game environment where a game player is provided a variety of vibrotactile sensations according to the road condition and the velocity of the player's car through a general model which generates vibrotactile signals (section 2).

4 Result and Evaluation

We conducted an experiment in order to verify the feasibility of the proposed game. 6 volunteers took part. Four were male, two female and they had an average age of

23.83. In the study, the subjects experienced the racing game without the proposed vibrotactile generation method for 2 minutes. Then they played the racing game with haptic feedback for 2 minutes. In each case, after playing the game, they were asked the following three questions:

a) Did you feel a variation of the car's velocity whenever you increased or decreased the velocity of the car?
b) Did you feel a sensation when the player's car was driven on the hard shoulder?
c) Did you feel the sensation when your car went over the bumps on the road?

For each question, subjects were required to answer either 'Yes' or 'No'. Table 1 shows the results. With the haptic feedback, all subjects answered that they felt the car's velocity change when they increased or decreased the velocity of the car. Even though they did not observe the graphical environment, they could haptically sense the car's speed. Furthermore, five out of the six subjects answered that they felt a haptic sensation as they drove a car on the hard shoulder and on the bump on the racing track. These results suggest that the proposed game provides realistic vibrotactile sensation in real-time.

Table 1. Comparison between the conventional game and the proposed game

		Game Type	
		Conventional Game (without haptic feedback)	Proposed Game (with haptic feedback)
Question	(a)	2/6	6/6
	(b)	0/6	5/6
	(c)	0/6	5/6

5   Conclusion

Past mobile games have been limited to including visual and audio feedback due to the absence of any systematic methods for generating vibrotactile signals. This paper proposed a racing game prototype which incorporated a vibrotactile signal generation method which can stimulate mechanoreceptors in a human somatosensory system. Unlike the conventional mobile game, the proposed racing game allowed players haptically sense a car's velocity and the state of a road surface. Through an experiment, we verified that the haptic feedback in the proposed game is shown to be realistic.

When we push a real accelerator pedal, the haptic sensation we experience alters according to the velocity of the car. In our game, acceleration is controlled by pushing a button. If the haptic sensation for pushing the button is changed according to the acceleration or velocity, a game player can haptically feel not only velocity but also the sensations of acceleration. Consequently, we are currently investigating a method which generates the above haptic sensation and hope to add further haptic realism to mobile gaming in our future work.

References

1. http://www.w3reports.com
2. Johansson, R.S., Vallbo, A.B.: Tactile sensibility in the human hand: relative and absolute densities of four types of mechanoreceptive units in glabrous skin. Journal of Physiology 286, 283–300 (1979)
3. Harrison, B.L., Fishkin, K.P., Gujar, A., Mochon, C., Want, R.: Squeeze Me, Hold Me, Tilt Me! An Exploration of Manipulative User Interfaces. In: CHI 1998. Conference on Human Factors in Computing Systems, pp. 17–24 (1998)
4. Kaaresoja, T., Linjama, J.: Perception of Short Tactile Pulses Generated by a Vibration Motor in a Mobile Phone. In: WHC 2005. First Joint Eurohaptics Conference and Symposium on Haptic Interfaces for Virtual Environment and Teleoperator Systems, pp. 471–472 (2005)
5. Chang, A., O'Modhrain, S., Jacob, R., Gunther, E., Ishii, H.: ComTouch: Design of a Vibrotactile Communication Device. In: ACM Designing Interactive Systems Conference, pp. 312–320 (2002)
6. Linjama, J., Häkkilä, J., Ronkainen, S.: Gesture Interfaces for Mobile Devices - Minimalist Approach for Haptic Interaction. In: CHI 2005. Conference on Human Factors in Computing Systems, portland (2005)
7. Oakley, I., Ängeslevä, J., Hughes, S., O'Modhrain, S.: Tilt and feel: scrolling with vibrotactile display. In: Eurohaptics 2004, pp. 316–323 (2004)
8. Oakley, I., O'Modhrain, S.: Tilt to Scroll: Evaluating a Motion Based Vibrotactile Mobile Interface. In: WHC 2005. First Joint Eurohaptics Conference and Symposium on Haptic Interfaces for Virtual Environment and Teleoperator Systems, pp. 40–49 (2005)
9. Sekiguchi, Y., Hirota, K., Hirose, M.: The Design and Implementation of Ubiquitous Haptic Device. In: WHC 2005. First Joint Eurohaptics Conference and Symposium on Haptic Interfaces for Virtual Environment and Teleoperator Systems, pp. 527–528 (2005)
10. Poupyrev, I., Maruyama, S., Rekimoto, J.: Ambient Touch: Designing Tactile Interfaces for Handheld Devices. In: 15th annual ACM Symposium on User Interface Software and Technology, pp. 51–60 (2002)
11. www.immersion.com/mobility/
12. Kim, S.Y., Kim, K.Y., Soh, B.S., Yang, G.Y., Kim, S.R.: Vibrotactile Rendering for Simulating Virtual Environment in a Mobile Game. IEEE Transaction on Consumer Electronics 52(4) (2006)

Obstacle Detection and Avoidance System
for Visually Impaired People

Byeong-Seok Shin[1] and Cheol-Su Lim[2]

[1] Department of Computer Science and Information Engineering, Inha University
253 Yonghyeon-Dong, Nam-Gu, Inchon, 402-751, Korea
bsshin@inha.ac.kr
[2] Department of Computer Engineering, Seokyeong University,
16-1 Jungneung-Dong, Sungbuk-Gu, Seoul 136-704, Korea
cslim@skuniv.ac.kr

Abstract. In this paper, we implemented a wearable system for visually impaired users which allows them to detect and avoid obstacles. This is based on ultrasound sensors which can acquire range data from objects in the environment by estimating the time-of-flight of the ultrasound signal. Using a hemispherical sensor array, we can detect obstacles and determine which directions should be avoided. However, the ultrasound sensors are only used to detect whether obstacles are present in front of users. We determine unimpeded directions by analyzing patterns of the range values from consecutive frames. Feedback is presented to users in the form of voice commands and vibration patterns. Our system is composed of an ARM9-based embedded system, an ultrasonic sensor array, an orientation tracker and a set of vibration motors with controller.

1 Introduction

Visually impaired people typically depend on a white cane or a guide dog whilst walking outdoors. Although a white cane is a simple and robust device, it has a disadvantage that it can only detect obstacles through making contact with them: its range is very short. A guide dog performs well for important tasks such as avoiding obstacles and basic navigation. However, it is arduous to train guide dogs, and they can be challenging and inconvenient for a visually impaired person to look after. To solve these problems, researchers have devised a variety of methods and systems to help visually impaired people.

The systems can be categorized as ETA (Electronic Travel Aids) or RTA (Robotic Travel Aids). ETAs are usually implemented as a portable system. Using a CCD camera, ETAs capture forward facing images and detect obstacles or find pathways using image processing techniques [1],[2]. However, this method requires a lot of computation, and can be slow. A second method relies on ultrasound sensors that acquire range data about the distances to obstacles [3],[4]. However, it does not consider the fact that the human body is subjected to many small movements while walking (trembling, rotations of the torso, undulations from stepping) and consequently data

I. Oakley and S. Brewster (Eds.): HAID 2007, LNCS 4813, pp. 78–85, 2007.
© Springer-Verlag Berlin Heidelberg 2007

captured from the sensors may change frequently. RTA uses mobile robots for active walk guidance [5], [6], [7]. Since this approach depends on the power and mobility of robots, the weight of the system is not critical and powerful computers can be used. However, such robots can only walk on relatively flat and smooth surfaces meaning their mobility is more restricted than wearable systems. Our system can be categorized as an ETA. We devise a computationally simple algorithm that can execute rapidly on light-weight and low performance devices. In addition, this system can detect small obstacles on the floor and objects hazardous to user's head.

In section 2, we explain our system in detail. In section 3, implementation details are discussed. Experimental results are presented in Sect.4. Finally, we close this paper by offering some conclusions.

2   Obstacles Detection and Avoidance System

Our system is composed of three parts: data gathering, data correction and orientation determination. In the data gathering step, we acquire spatial data from the environment with a specially-designed ultrasound sensor array and an orientation tracker. This combination of sensors provides not only range data to obstacles but also the orientation of the body (that is, the orientation of sensor array). Since the ultrasound sensors acquire surrounding noise as well as range data, we have to remove this in the data correction step. At the same time, we exploit the orientation tracker to estimate the posture of a user and determine whether the range value of current frame is valid or not. Lastly, we determine and present an appropriate direction for travel in orientation determination step.

2.1   Data Gathering

An ultrasound sensor acquires range data from the sensor to an object by estimating the time-of-flight of an ultrasound signal. When a series of range value decreases during walking, we can conclude that a potentially hazardous object is located on the user's path and they should change direction. Since a visually impaired person moves forward relatively rapidly, we have to obtain range information about the environment in front of the user frequently (at least 2~3 times per second). Therefore we use a set of ultrasound sensors arranged into an array. Each one points in a different direction and the coverage of its conic line of sight that does not overlap with those of neighboring sensors. In total, eight ultrasound sensors are arranged into three rows. The top row has two sensors, angled to detect objects hazardous to the user's head. The middle row has four sensors to accurately identify a safe navigation path. Finally, the bottom row has two sensors angle downwards to recognize small obstacles on the floor. Figure 1 shows the layout of sensors in our system. Although the sensor array is quite large, it has the advantage of guaranteeing high-speed range sensing since it employs many sensors in parallel. Needless to say, the size of the array is dependent on the physical characteristics of each sensor (size, weight, signal coverage and so on). In this system, the range data are gathered and sent to a wearable computer through a USB interface.

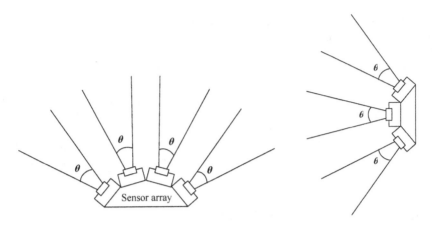

Fig. 1. Horizontal (left) and vertical (right) layout of ultrasound sensors in our system

2.2 Data Correction

Ultrasound sensors are cheap (compared to alternatives such as laser range scanners) and harmless, making them ideally suited to this domain. However, they are normally only used to detect whether obstacles are located in front of user or not, and are sensitive to spatial noise due to the mirror effect. Since the range values can therefore decrease or increase abruptly due to these kinds of noise, distance values between two consecutive frames can be quite divergent. To deal with this issue, we categorize as an outlier any sensor data that differs from the previous captured data by more than a set value. The value can be regarded as the maximum amount of movement that can take place in a single frame and was determined in the experiments described in section 4.

Another problem is that inaccurate range values can be gathered due to the fact that the user moves around continuously. For instance, when the user bends his or her body (perhaps during stepping) or trembles, the sensors may be pointing in the wrong direction and therefore obtain an incorrect range value. Such interfering readings need to be detected and prevented from contributing to the determination of valid movement directions. To ensure accurate scanning of the environment, we use an orientation tracker to estimate body movement. Based on this, our system makes a decision whether to use the range value of current frame or not. This is achieved by taking a reading from the orientation tracker whenever range data are transferred from ultra sound sensors. From this data, we can calculate the difference between the pitch and roll angles found in the current and previous frames. If this difference is larger than a set threshold value, the current range data are not considered by our obstacle avoidance algorithm. Fig. 2 illustrates the method used to detect invalid motions of the user's body.

2.3 Orientation Determination

Previous methods for path generation are algorithmically complex and require substantial computation to generate local and global maps of the environment in a

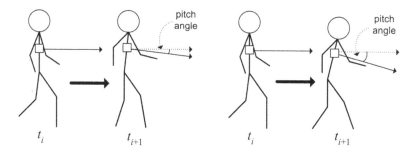

Fig. 2. This image shows the verification of the range data by considering the orientation of the sensor array. When the pitch angle between a direction of i-th scanning and that of $i+1$-th scanning is small, the range value is regarded as valid one (left), otherwise, it is ignored (right).

preprocessing step and also require extra storage for this spatial information [8], [9], [10]. In order to assist a user's walk-through using a low-performance mobile computer, the navigation method should be sufficiently simple that it can reach a decision in real-time and with only simple computation. Equally, it should not depend on large scale storage.

In the system described in this paper, the ultrasound sensors are arranged in three rows. The four sensors of middle row detect obstacles in front of users. In order to determine the direction to move in to avoid a collision, we construct a spatial structure from patterns of the range data. The range data from the four sensors is classified into four cases: danger, warning, adequate, and not considered. We can define input 256 cases (four sensors and four levels: 4^4) and then predefine a set direction response for each case. The case values and corresponding directions can be stored in a lookup table. While a user is walking in real space, we construct a bit code representing the case recorded on the sensors and retrieve the direction of avoidance by simply referring to the lookup table. This requires minimal processing and storage.

We also have to consider the local minima problem. In a cul-de-sac or blind alley, the direction recommended by this simple algorithm oscillates between left and right repeatedly. To resolve this issue, we use a heuristic based on the directions recommended in previous frames. Basically, if the direction recommended by the current frame is the reverse of that in the previous frame, the direction is left unchanged. Since visually impaired users move slowly, spatial structures are relatively stationary. Consequently, if we change the orientation of the recommended direction in current frame, we may select the direction of previous frame in the next frame.

Computed directions are displayed to users by means of voice commands and vibration patterns. They are quantized into four directions and mapped to voice messages or vibration patterns representing "rotate-left", "turn-left", "turn-right", and "rotate-right". Using a vibration jacket helps a user to understand the direction instinctively. We present additional commands such as "start", "stop", "watch your step", and "take care of your head" according to corresponding situations.

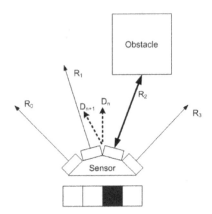

Fig. 3. Calculation of a recommended avoidance direction from a pattern of range data

3   System Implementation

Fig. 4 shows the configuration of prototype system. Eight ultrasound sensors are arranged with three rows. The top row has two sensors to detect objects hazardous to

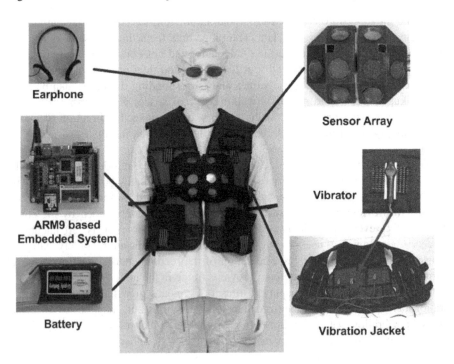

Fig. 4. System Configuration. It is composed of an ARM9-based embedded board with a Li-ion battery, the ultrasound sensor array and its controller, a vibration jacket with 8 vibrators, and a set of earphones.

user's head, the middle row has four sensors to compute a safe path to the target point, and the bottom row has two sensors to recognize small obstacles on the floor. The number of sensors is a trade-off between the manufacturing cost (and size) of the sensor array and its accuracy. We conclude that eight sensors are sufficient for this application by conducting an experiment. In this study, the output of the system takes the form of a series of voice commands.

4 Experimental Results

Evaluation of our system was performed in a corridor with several obstacles. Three users, of varying builds and body types, participated in our experiment. The eight ultrasound sensors gathered spatial information from the front of users 3~4 times per second and the user moved at a speed of about 1 meter per second. Fig. 5 shows the relationship between a real space and spatial information acquired by the sensor array as a user navigates. The gray region signifies the region covered by the ultrasound signal and the red curve is actual path walked. The experimental results show that our system can guide a user along a safe path even in a narrow corridor including several obstacles.

Fig. 6 depicts photographs which show a participant using the system to escape from a local minima, or dead end. Essentially, at the end of corridor, the user changes his orientation to the opposite direction, and returns to his original position.

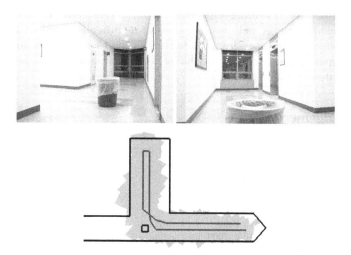

Fig. 5. Accuracy estimation of our system. The top row of images shows the environment where the experiment took place, a narrow corridor strewn with several obstacles. The bottom image is the local map generated by our system. The gray region signifies the coverage of ultrasound signal, and illustrates that our system can detect obstacles with a low error rate. The red line depicts the actual path taken by one of the participants and shows that they can success-fully return to their original position without colliding with obstacles or losing their way.

Fig. 6. An example of a user escaping from a local minimum. The user reverses his walking direction when confronted with a dead end.

5 Conclusion

We implemented a system that allows visually impaired users to detect and avoid obstacles as they walk around. Using a hemi-spherical sensor array, our system is able to accurately acquire spatial information. The sensor array is arranged in three rows. The top row has two sensors to detect objects hazardous to a user's head, the middle row has four sensors to determine a safe path and the bottom row has two sensors to identify small obstacles on the floor. We detect potentially confounding changes to the alignment of the user's body with an orientation tracker, and use this input to make a decision as to whether or not to use the range value captured in the current frame. We also solve the local minima problem by comparing previous directions with the current recommended direction.

Future work will concentrate on improving the performance of our method. Although our method works well in flat regions, it is difficult to apply it to detect descending staircases and other drop-offs in front of the user. As these are potentially dangerous environmental features, extending our system to deal with them is an important direction for future research.

Acknowledgements

This work was supported by IITA through IT Leading R&D Support Project.

References

1. Molton, N., Se, S., Lee, D., Brady, M., Probert, P.: Robotic Sensing for the Guidance of the Visually Impaired. In: FSR 1997. Proceedings of International Conference on Field and Service Robotics, pp. 236–243 (1997)
2. Ferrari, F., Grosso, E., Sandini, G., Magrassi, M.: A stereo vision system for real time obstacle avoidance in unknown environment. In: Proceedings of IEEE International Workshop on IntelligentRobots and Systems, pp. 703–708. IEEE Computer Society Press, Los Alamitos (1990)
3. Borenstein, J.: The NavBelt - A Computerized Multi-Sensor Travel Aid for Active Guidance of the Blind. In: Proceedings of the CSUN's Fifth Annual Conference on Technology and Persons with Disabilities, pp. 107–116 (1990)

4. Borenstein, J., Koren, Y.: Obstacle Avoidance With Ultrasonic Sensors. IEEE Journal of Robotics and Automation, RA4(2), 213–218 (1988)
5. Mori, H., Kotani, S.: Robotic travel aid for the blind: HARUNOBU-6. In: Proc. 2nd Euro. Conf. Disability, Virtual Reality & Assoc. Tech., pp. 193–202 (1998)
6. Borenstein, J., Ulrich, I.: The GuideCane: A Computerized Travel Aid for the Active Guidance of Blind Pedestrians. In: Proceedings of the IEEE International Conference on Robotics and Automation, pp. 1283–1288 (1997)
7. Shim, H.M., Lee, J.S., Lee, E.H., Hong, S.H.: A Study on the Sound-Imaging Algorithm of Obstacle Information for the Visually Impaired. In: ITC-CSCC 2002, pp. 389–392 (2002)
8. Jiang, K., Seveviratine, L.D., Earles, S.W.E.: A Shortest Path Based Path Planning Algorithm for Nonholonomic Mobile Robots. Journal of Intelligent and Robotic Systems, 347–366 (1999)
9. Divelbiss, A.W., Wen, J.T.: A Path Space Approach to Nonholonomic Motion Planning in the Presence of Obstacles. IEEE Transactions on Robotics and Automation 13(3), 443–451 (1997)
10. Hu, H., Gu, D., Brady, M.: Navigation and Guidance of An Intelligent Mobile Robot. In: EUROBOT 1997. Second Euromicro Workshop on Advanced Mobile Robots, pp. 104–111 (1997)

Tangible User Interface for the Exploration of Auditory City Maps

Martin Pielot[1], Niels Henze[1], Wilko Heuten[1], and Susanne Boll[2]

[1] OFFIS Institute for Information Technology, Escherweg 2, 26121 Oldenburg, Germany
{Pielot,Henze,Heuten}@offis.de
[2] University of Oldenburg, Escherweg 2, 26121 Oldenburg, Germany
Susanne.boll@informatik.uni-oldenburg.de

Abstract. Before venturing out into unfamiliar areas, most people scope out a map. But for the blind or visually impaired traditional maps are not accessible. In our previous work, we developed the "Auditory Map" which conveys the location of geographic objects through spatial sonification. Users perceive these objects through the virtual listener's ears walking through the presented area. Evaluating our system we observed that the participants had difficulties perceiving the directions of geographic objects accurately. To improve the localization we introduce rotation to the Auditory Map. Rotation is difficult to achieve with traditional input devices such as a mouse or a digitizer tablet. This paper describes a tangible user interface which allows rotating the virtual listener using physical representations of the map and the virtual listener. First evaluation results show that our interaction technique is a promising approach to improve the construction of cognitive maps for visually impaired people.

Keywords: sonification, auditory display, tangible user interface, spatial audio, exploration, interaction techniques, visually impaired users.

1 Introduction

The ability to travel is an important factor for social inclusion. Traveling to unknown areas relies on external information resources like city maps, which can be utilized at home during the travel preparation. Blind people are mostly not able to access these representations. Consequently, they usually do not travel to unknown areas and are excluded from many social activities. We developed "Auditory Map" which conveys geographic information to blind and visually impaired people through an auditory display [6, 7]. We identified the geographic entities that are most important to gain an overview of an area like lakes, parks, and buildings. They are represented by continuously playing corresponding natural sounds such as dabbling water or singing birds. These sounds are placed on a plane within a virtual sound room according to their locations on the map thus maintaining their spatial relations. Users walk through the room virtually by moving a virtual listener. The sound objects transmit their sound up to a maximum distance, so that the user perceives the sounds of the objects in the near environment of the virtual listener only. A lake on the left of the virtual listener is heard from the left and a lake on the right is heard from the right. A digitizer tablet

I. Oakley and S. Brewster (Eds.): HAID 2007, LNCS 4813, pp. 86–97, 2007.

serves as input device for the exploration. The city map is mapped on the tablet, which thus represents an absolute frame of reference. Moving the stylus over the tablet updates the virtual listener's position accordingly (see Figure 1).

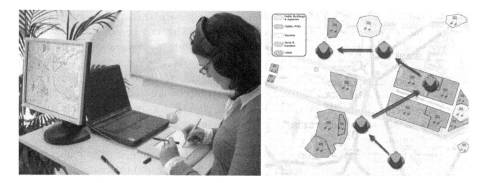

Fig. 1. A user exploring an area with the Auditory Map

Our previous evaluations [6, 7] of the Auditory Map with blind and sighted participants showed that the exploration of auditory maps leads to survey knowledge about the presented area and to the ability of making spatial decisions. Nevertheless, we identified difficulties localizing auditory objects that occur in particular when objects are in front or behind of the virtual listener. This can be solved by enabling the user to rotate the virtual listener within the virtual sound room. However, the currently used digitizer tablet cannot serve as input device for rotating.

In this paper we therefore describe a newly developed tangible user interface for the exploration of virtual sound rooms. It combines the advantages of a digitizer tablet and its stylus with the possibility to rotate the virtual listener continuously. We assume that this interface will improve the access to the sound rooms' information for blind and visually impaired people, leading to more accurate mental representations of spatial information and providing more confidence in making spatial decisions.

In the following section, we analyze the causes of localization difficulties and ways to address them. Section 3 discusses the related work. Section 4 proposes the new tangible user interface for exploring virtual sound rooms followed by the description of its implementation using computer vision technology in Section 5. The preliminary evaluation of the tangible user interface is presented in Section 6. We close this paper with a summary and an outlook.

2 Reasons for Localization Inaccuracy

The Auditory Map uses an auditory display to convey geographic information. Auditory objects are arranged in a planar sound room, rendered by a 3D sound library, and conveyed using headphones. To build a realistic mental map of the presented area it is important to localize the geographic objects accurately. Localization accuracy is affected by certain aspects that we will highlight in this section. We also outline our concept to improve the localization accuracy by introducing rotation to the Auditory Map.

Evaluating our Auditory Map [6, 7] we observed that our participants had difficulties to perceive the directions of geographic objects accurately. We found three reasons for that:

1. Localization accuracy of sound sources is limited even in the real world due to limitations of the human perception [1] and in particular in virtual sound rooms [4] due to limitations of the acoustic rendering. This can be countered by using personalized spatial audio displays but is not feasible for applications that address a broader audience.
2. The sounds used to display geographic objects are important for localization accuracy. In Auditory Maps, geographic objects are represented by natural sounds. This limits the number of possible choices for the representing sounds. Thus sounds might have to be chosen which are not ideal from the perspective of localization accuracy.
3. The lack of context information in virtual sound rooms compared to reality leads to more front-back confusions [18]. In reality we move and rotate our head while listening to a sound source. We are thus able to combine the knowledge about the head's movement with the changing acoustic impression and construct a more accurate spatial model of the sound sources' locations.

To improve the localization inaccuracy we address this lack of context information. Minnaar et al. have shown that head movements can reduce the localization blur when listening to synthesized spatial sound [12]. Head movement also helps avoiding front-back confusion [10]. We therefore will enable the user to rotate the virtual listener continuously as if it would turn its head left and right. If the user is not sure whether an auditory object is behind or in front, he or she can rotate the listener and follow the movement of the sound source. The user can resolve front-back confusions in a self-directed way. However, the digitizer tablet is not suitable to alter the orientation of the listener. Thus, the interaction with the Auditory Map has to be revised. The following section will review existing work on which we based our design decisions.

3   Related Work

Sleuth [5] and AudioDoom [9] use a virtual listener to explore spatial audio information. The interaction is realized by a mouse and a ringmouse. Both input devices provide no frame of reference. To avoid the possible loss of orientation the freedom of interaction is restricted to 90° steps. Since we aim at continuous rotation, this solution is not appropriate for the Auditory Map. The Nomadic Radio [14] by Sawhney and Schmandt utilizes speech recognition to manage voice and text-based messages with an auditory display. Cohen [3] proposed a gesture-based interface, where users could point, catch and drag spatially arranged sounds. Both methods are not suitable for our task because they do not provide feedback about the virtual listener's position and orientation.

Tangible user interfaces enable users to interact with digital information systems over tangible physical artifacts. Each physical artifact represents and allows manipulation of the digital information it is associated with [16]. Thus, the physical artifacts provide haptic feedback about the associated digital states. The ActiveCube of

Watanabe et al. [17] has shown that tangible user interfaces are well suited to convey spatial information to visually impaired and blind people. The project Tangible Newspaper [15] shows, that tangible user interfaces are also well suited for obtaining an overview about complex documents such as maps. Boverman et al. [2] did promising research at exploring spatially sonified information with tangible user interfaces. They allow users to scan the information by "exciting" them with a physical artifact. These projects indicate that tangible user interfaces are well applicable for the exploration of the sound room used in the Auditory Map.

4 A Tangible User Interface for Exploring Virtual Sound Rooms

Exploiting the previously discussed advantages, we developed a novel user interface to integrate rotation into the Auditory Map. We did not use the user's head movement to rotate the listener of a virtual acoustic room since that would divide the control of position and orientation into two modalities. It would also require the user to perform 360° turns. However, as we use the position of the Auditory Map stylus input device to move the virtual listener we could also use the orientation of the input device to adjust the orientation of the virtual listener.

The interaction technique based on the digitizer tablet was highly appreciated by our users. We assume that the characteristics of this technique are a good guideline to develop an interaction that enables the user to move and rotate the virtual listener. In the following section we analyze the requirements for the enhanced interaction. Afterwards we determine the physical artifacts for the tangible user interface and design the user interaction.

4.1 Requirements

When exploring a map, position and orientation of the virtual listener are not displayed explicitly by the auditory display. This lack of feedback can lead to the loss of orientation as described by Ohuchi et al. [13]. It would also become more likely that the user cannot distinguish between self-motion and movement of the perceived objects [8]. When using the digitizer tablet to interact with the Auditory Map the tablet serves as a frame of reference since the relation between the surface and the stylus translates directly to the position of the virtual listener in relation to the border of the presented map. This allows the user to haptically identify the virtual listener's current position. For introducing rotation a similar frame of reference, haptic feedback, and intuitive mapping is needed. We identified the following five requirements. The tangible user interface has to:

- enable the user to place the virtual listener at any location on the displayed map,
- enable the user to continuously rotate the virtual listener around the vertical axis,
- provide feedback about the virtual listener's position,
- provide feedback about the virtual listener's orientation, and
- provide this feedback immediately.

4.2 Determining the Artifacts

Regarding these requirements we concluded that the map and the virtual listener need to be represented as physical artifacts. To determine appropriate physical artifacts Ullmer and Ishii describe three common approaches [16]: Their least favorable approach subordinates aesthetical aspects to technical issues. The artifact is chosen by its functionality and not because it suites well from the perspective of usability and design. Their most favorable approach is the augmentation of existing physical artifacts while retaining their typical usage. This allows people to apply their existing knowledge to the new interface. Their third approach uses so called "found objects" and is favorable if the previous approach is not applicable. If the right objects are chosen, the user can suggest their functionality by their appearance.

Choosing the physical representation for the map we followed the second approach. We took a tactile map as archetype and identified the paper on which the map is printed as the complement to the map of the auditory displayed map. Instead of a paper sheet we chose a felt pad as the physical representation of the map because its borders are easier to perceive haptically. The size of the pad shown in Figure 2 is about 16x12 inches (40x30 cm). We marked the northern border with an adhesive strip to make the cardinal directions identifiable by touch.

Since the virtual listener is a unique feature of the Auditory Map, the choice of a physical artifact is not as straight-forward as for the map. Common tactile maps are explored by the user's finger. Following the preferred approach the user's finger would serve as representation for the virtual listener. But when exploring tactile maps the orientation of the finger does not alter the perception of the map in the way rotation would alter the perception of the auditory display. In addition, using the finger would require uneconomical gestures of a user. Thus we decided against using the user's finger for the interaction. Instead we used a "found object". For the prototype we chose a toy duck, which is shown in Figure 2. Due to the characteristic physique of ducks, visually impaired users can determine its orientation by touching it.

Fig. 2. Exploring the Auditory Map by moving and rotating the virtual listener's artifact

Users explore the Auditory Map by moving and rotating the duck while it is located on top of the pad. The position and orientation of both artifacts in relation to each other is transferred immediately to the virtual listener's position and orientation. Users can rotate the duck and the pad to change the orientation of the virtual listener. For example, if the virtual listener's artifact is located in the south western corner of the pad and faces the eastern border, the virtual listener is placed in the south western corner of the map, and turned eastwards. If the user moves the virtual listener's artifact to the middle of the pad and turns it north, the virtual listener does the same movement (see Figure 2). This enables the user to determine position and orientation of the virtual listener inside the map by examining the state of the tangible user interface.

5 Implementation

The concept described in the previous section has been realized by implementing the tangible user interface and integrating it with the existing Auditory Map. In order to make the tangible user interface work, it has to track the position and orientation of the physical artifacts that represents the map and the virtual listener. Tracking the artifacts must be performed with short latency. In order to build a reliable and low-cost system we decided to use computer vision technology based on inexpensive webcams. We implemented the visual object tracking using and extending the Intel Open Source Computer Vision Library (OpenCV). The artifacts' relative positions and orientations are used to calculate the virtual listener's position and orientation inside the map. We assume that the webcam is mounted perpendicular to the pad artifact and the virtual listener's artifact is on top of the pad.

5.1 Follow the Map Artifact

To track the position and orientation of the pad we implemented a three-stage process that takes place after calibrating the algorithm. First, we separate the artifact from the background, then we identify the artifact using previous knowledge about its size and shape, and finally we determine its position and orientation. Figure 3 shows the image of the webcam on the left and the recognized position of the map's artifact after background subtraction in the centre.

Prior to using the tangible user interface the setup has to be prepared by putting the pad into the area captured by the webcam. The system recognizes the pad by its rectangular shape and assumes that the artifact's current top edge symbolize the north-edge of the map. To separate the artifact from the background we implemented a non-adaptive background subtraction [11]. This technique compares a static prepared image of the background pixel-wise with current images of the camera. If the difference between a pair of pixels is greater than a certain threshold the pixel is considered as a part of foreground objects. The other pixels are considered to be background and turned black. In the resulting foreground image the algorithm looks for edges that form connected graphs. Graphs without at least one pair of orthogonal edges are discarded. Pairs of orthogonal edges are being used trying to approximate the pose of the artifact by taking the artifact's position detected in the previous video frame into account. Finally, the cardinal directions of the edges are determined by comparing the artifact's position and orientation with the previous position and orientation. The algorithm is robust against occlusion as long as one edge is completely visible and one of its adjacent edges one is visible.

5.2 Track the Virtual Listener's Artifact

While users interact with the tangible user interface the listener's artifact will always be in front of the map's artifact. Thus, it can not be identified as a single object using background subtraction. Since we do not want to restrict the choice of the artifact for the virtual listener, we also cannot utilize knowledge about its shape as we did with the map. Hence, we choose a tracking method that is independent from background subtraction and the artifact's shape. The chosen method relies on markers to track the artifact's position and orientation. The artifact has to be tagged with two specific markers as shown in the right of Figure 3. One marker is fixed at the front and the other at the back of the artifact. The markers are identified by the hue with must be unique. The algorithm searches for pixels with each marker's hue. Afterwards, the center of the found pixels is calculated. By using the vector between the centers of each centers, as indicated by the line in the right of Figure 3, the position and orientation of the artifact is determined. Once the system is calibrated to the markers' hue, the detection runs stable and recovers quickly from distractions like temporary occlusion of the artifact.

Fig. 3. Tracking the map's artifact (left and centre) and marker-based detection of the virtual listener's position and orientation (right)

6 Evaluation

We conducted a preliminary evaluation with the implemented tangible user interface. We gathered quantitative and qualitative data by conducting three experiments and afterwards handing out questionnaires to the participants. The goal was to get indications about whether rotation and the tangible user interface are useful extension to the Auditory Map.

6.1 Evaluation Setup and Methods

The evaluation was performed by eight sighted participants. All of them were between 16 and 35 years old. No one had previous experience with the Auditory Map or the tangible user interface. All participants were sighted but blindfolded prior to the evaluation. Thus they had to make themselves familiar with the system without vision. We assume that sighted blindfolded users are well suited to provide preliminary feedback about the tangible user interface. Later evaluations will be conducted with the target user group.

Figure 4 shows the system setup that was used during the evaluation. The left image shows the setup of the webcam that was mounted on a holder perpendicular to a table below. The center image shows a participant interacting with the tangible user interface. The right image shows the map used in the second and the third experiment. The lake is represented by dabbling water, the park by singing birds, the church by the sound of church bells, and the visitor attraction by the noise of several single-lens reflex cameras. The dashed lines indicate the route that should be followed in the one of the experiments.

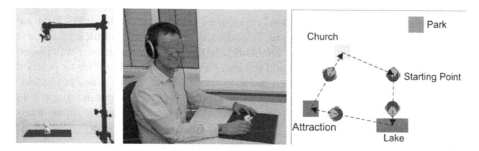

Fig. 4. System setup (left), a user interacting with the tangible user interface (center), and scheme of the map used in the experiments (right)

We used protocol sheets, a photo camera and a video camera to log the experiments, their results and the participant's notes. The protocol sheets were used to write down the results of each experiment and the annotations made by the participants. The state of the tangible user interface during the experiments was recorded with the photo camera. The video camera was used to monitor the participant's interaction with the tangible user interface during the experiments for later analyses. Following the experiments we handed out questionnaires to the participants. They contained multiple choice questions where the participants could rate aspects of the tangible user interface. Further open questions encouraged the participants to write down their impressions, considerations and suggestions.

6.2 Experiments and Results

During the evaluation we conducted three experiments. The experiments should evaluate whether the tangible user interface acts as a frame of reference, whether rotation helps to increase the localization accuracy and whether rotation as an interaction technique is accepted by the users.

Experiment 1. The first experiment should show if the tangible user interface serves as a frame of reference for the position and orientation of the listener. It consisted of two tasks. The first task was to determine the listener's orientation, which was placed randomly on the map before. The second task was to place it exactly at the center of the map and align it exactly north. The experiment was conducted without the auditory output of the Auditory Map. Since the participants were blindfolded, they had to rely solely on their sense of touch.

The deviation of the listener's orientation the participants determined in the first task averaged 1.6°. In the second task, the deviation of the alignment with the north-south axis averaged 5.5°. The deviation of the listener's position from the map's center averaged 2.0% east-west and 4.3% north-south of the map artifact's size. The results show that users can determine the listener's position and orientation with only slight deviations. The experiment showed that it is easy for users to determine the position and the orientation of the listener through the haptic sense only when interacting with the tangible user interface. Thus the tangible user interface can serve as the frame of reference.

Experiment 2. The goal of the second experiment was to examine the impact of rotation on the localization of landmarks. It consisted of two tasks and took place on a map (see Figure 4) containing four landmarks. In the first task the listener was placed at the map's center, aligned north and the users were not allowed to alter its position and orientation. The participants then had to estimate the direction of three landmarks. In the second task, they were encouraged to rotate the listener without moving it And re-estimating the directions of the three landmarks. Comparing the directions determined during the two tasks should show whether rotation helps to improve the localization accuracy and helps to resolve front-back confusions.

The results of the second experiment differed significantly depending on the sound of the landmark, the users were asked to localize. The localization of the lake showed that rotation can help in overcoming uncertainties of localizing landmarks. Without rotation five of the eight participants were not certain of the lake's direction. With rotation every participant was able to estimate a direction. Nevertheless we still observed front-back confusions in two cases. Every participant was able to localize the church. The comparison of the average deviations with and without rotation showed that rotation improves the accuracy of determining it direction. The deviation of the directions given by the participants was reduced to 15.4° and a median of 10° with rotation, compared to 27.75° average and a median of 25° without rotation. The localization of the park showed the importance to choose well distinguishable sounds for landmarks when allowing rotation. All participants stated that they had problems to distinguish the park's bird chanting from the camera noise of the attraction. Without rotation allowed, two of the eight participants were uncertain about the park's location. With rotation allowed four participants could not locate the park. The results of the second experiment indicated that rotation improves the localization of landmarks only if their sound can be easily distinguished from the other landmarks' sounds.

Experiment 3. The third experiment should show whether rotation is accepted by the users and represents a valuable enhancement of the interaction with the Auditory Map. We wanted to observe, if users make use of rotation spontaneously. The participants were asked to follow and describe a route between four landmarks (see Figure 4). They were asked to determine the relative direction changes along from the perspective of a person that walks along this route. This task should implicitly encourage the participants to use rotation.

While exploring the route, the participants were allowed to interact with the interface without restrictions. The video camera was used to record the participants' interaction while accomplishing the task. The videos were used to analyze if and how rotation was used to follow and describe the route. All participants were all able to give the direction changes with little deviation. All participants rotated the listener spontaneously to localize subsequent landmarks and to determine the relative direction change. This indicates that rotation is well accepted and found valuable by the users.

Overall user observations. To get an idea about the participants' impression we analyzed the questionnaires and the participant's notes. Most participants found it easy to determine position and orientation of the listener in the first experiment. In the second experiment most of them found it hard to localize landmarks, especially without rotation. Although rotation only improved the localization of the church and the lake, most participants noted that rotation eased the localization of landmarks for them. They also found rotation useful for following the route in third experiment. Many participants stated that localizing the park and the lake was difficult, while localizing the attraction and the church was easy due to their respective sounds. Many participants found the tangible user interface easy to understand. One participant stated that the duck especially helped to determine the relative direction changes. Some participants found it difficult to concentrate on the task while listening to the auditory presentation of the map and proposed to make the volume adjustable. The participants only rotated by turning the listener's artifact, not the map's artifact. Most users localized landmarks by turning the listener's artifact until facing it.

6.3 Discussion

Since the participants found rotation useful and spontaneously made use of it during the third experiment, we assume that rotation is a useful enhancement of the interaction with the Auditory Map. The localization of the well distinguishable sounds improved with rotation while the localization of the badly distinguishable sounds did not. This indicates the importance to choose easily distinguishable sounds to represent landmarks. Rotation has also been used to resolve uncertainties and front-back confusions, though they were not always resolved correctly. We assume that the front-back confusions that occur with rotation were due to the participants' lack of experience.

Even though we observed uncertainties and front-back confusion with rotation, none of the participants lost orientation during the evaluation. This indicates that the tangible user interface is a well suited frame of reference. The participants had no problems to interact with the Auditory Map even though they had not seen the tangible user interface prior to the experiments. The participants found the tangible user interface easy to understand and showed no problems to interact with the Auditory Map.

7 Conclusions

In this paper we presented a novel tangible user interface for the exploration of virtual sound rooms by moving and rotating a virtual listener through them. We integrated it into our previous work, the Auditory Map, which utilizes spatial non-speech sound to present geographic entities and their spatial relations. The user interface consists of two physical artifacts representing the map and the virtual listener. Blind users now simply interact with the Auditory Map by moving and rotating physical objects. These manipulations are tracked by computer vision technology and are mapped accordingly to the virtual listener and map.

Our evaluation showed that the physical objects provide immediate feedback to the user about the virtual listener's location and orientation on the map. We observed that the participants intensively used rotation and that they found rotation very helpful to determine the direction of the geographic objects. We assume that the tangible user interface would be even more effective for trained users. The combination of presenting information through spatial sound and using tangible user interfaces to explore this information has great potential to provide access to any spatially distributed data. In the future further evaluations with the target user group will be conducted. Another aspect of our further research will be to advance the tangible user interface by integrating panning and zooming into auditory maps.

References

1. Blauert, J.: Spatial Hearing: The psychophysics of human sound localization. MIT Press, Cambridge (1999)
2. Bovermann, T., Hermann, T., Ritter, H.: Tangible Data Scanning Sonification Model. In: Conference on Auditory Display (2006)
3. Cohen, M.: Throwing, pitching and catching sound: audio windowing models and modes. International Journal of Man-Machine Studies 39(2), 269–304 (1993)
4. Donker, H., Klante, P., Gorny, P.: The design of auditory user interfaces for blind users. In: Nordic conference on Human-computer interaction (2002)
5. Drewes, T., Mynatt, E., Gandy, M.: Sleuth: An Audio Experience. In: International Conference on Auditory Display (2000)
6. Heuten, W., Henze, N., Boll, S.: Interactive Exploration of City Maps with Auditory Torches. In: Computer-Human Interaction (2007)
7. Heuten, W., Wichmann, D., Boll, S.: Interactive 3D Sonification for the Exploration of City Maps. In: Proceedings of the 4th Nordic conference on Human-computer interaction (2006)
8. Larsson, P., Västfjäll, D., Kleiner, M.: Perception of Self-motion and Presence in Auditory Virtual Environments. In: Conference on Auditory Display (2004)
9. Lumbreras, M., Sánchez, J.: Interactive 3D sound hyperstories for blind children. In: Computer/Human Interaction Conference (1999)
10. Marentakis, G., Brewster, S.A: Gesture Interaction with Spatial Audio Displays: Effects of Target Size and Inter-Target Separation. In: Conference on Auditory Display (2005)
11. McIvor, A.M.: Background subtraction techniques. In: Proceedings of Image and Vision Computing (2000)
12. Minnaar, P., Olesen, S.K., Christensen, F., Møller, H.: The Importance of Head Movements for Binaural Room Synthesis. In: Conference on Auditory Display (2001)
13. Ohuchi, M., Iwaya, Y., Suzuki, Y., Munekata, T.: Cognitive-map Formation of Blind Persons in a Virtual Sound Environment. In: Conference on Auditory Display (2006)
14. Sawhney, N., Schmandt, C.: Nomadic radio: scaleable and contextual notification for wearable audio messaging. In: Computer-Human Interaction Conference (1999)
15. Sporka, A.J., Němec, V., Slavík, P.: Tangible newspaper for the visually impaired users. In: Computer/Human Interaction Conference (2005)

16. Ullmer, B., Ishii, H.: Emerging frameworks for tangible interfaces. IBM Systems Journal 39(3-4), 915–931 (2000)
17. Watanabe, R., Itoh, Y., Asai, M., Kitamura, Y., Kishino, F., Kikuchi, H.: The soul of ActiveCube: implementing a flexible, multimodal, three-dimensional spatial tangible interface. Computers in Entertainment 2(4), 15–15 (2004)
18. Wightman, F.L., Kistler, D.J.: Resolution of front-back ambiguity in spatial hearing by listener and source movement. Journal of the Acoustical Society of America 105(5), 2841–2853 (1999)

Haptic and Sound Grid for Enhanced Positioning in a 3-D Virtual Environment

Seung-Chan Kim and Dong-Soo Kwon

Human Robot Interaction Research Center, KAIST
335 Gwahangno, Yuseong-gu, Daejon 305-701, Republic of Korea
kimsc@robot.kaist.ac.kr, kwonds@kaist.ac.kr
http://robot.kaist.ac.kr

Abstract. As images are projected onto the flat retina when identifying objects scattered in space, there may be considerable ambiguity in depth (i.e. z-direction) perception. Therefore, position information can be distorted, especially along the z-axis. In this paper, virtual grids using haptic and auditory feedback are proposed to complement ambiguous visual depth cues. This study experimentally investigates the influence of virtual grids on position identification in a 3-D workspace. A haptic grid is generated using the PHANTOM® Omni™ and a sound grid is generated by changing the frequency characteristics of the sound source based on the hand movement of the operator. Both grids take the form of virtual planes placed at regular intervals of 10mm through three axes (i.e. x, y, and z). The haptic and sound grids are conveyed to subjects separately or simultaneously according to test conditions. In cases of bimodal presentation, the grids are displayed with cross-modal synchrony. The statistically significant results indicate that the presence of the grid in space increased the average values of precision. In particular, errors in the z-axis decreased by more than 50% (F=19.82, p<0.01).

Keywords: grid plane, depth ambiguity, haptic, auditory, multimodality.

1 Introduction

An interface is a physical device or a virtual system that enables humans, or other subjects, to communicate with one another. During a task involving manual exploration or navigation in three-dimensional (3D) spaces there is inevitably a lack of position information, because depth information mainly originates from perspective cues. This is shown in Fig. 1. The difficulties that lead to errors in point-to-point movements in 3D spaces brings about the necessity of a grid which supports location awareness, typically made up of a series of intersecting vertical and horizontal lines. From the viewpoint of spatial awareness, the application of a grid is expected to enhance task efficiency in a 3D workspace, in a manner akin to its utility in object alignment in the case of a 2D space.

To enhance the effectiveness of an interface, grids that allow more precision in positioning have been proposed. Fig. 2 shows a schematic of a grid. However,

I. Oakley and S. Brewster (Eds.): HAID 2007, LNCS 4813, pp. 98–109, 2007.
© Springer-Verlag Berlin Heidelberg 2007

Fig. 1. Schematic of movement in a virtual environment

because the visual grid plane may prevent users from seeing already existing visual information, only non-visual feedback, i.e. haptic and auditory feedback, is implemented in the form of a plane, that is, a virtual grid plane.

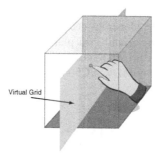

Virtual Grid

Fig. 2. Schematic of a virtual grid

For human computer interaction (HCI), a mouse is generally utilized as a 2D graphic user interface. Because the visual-only interactions limit the ease with which users can interact with computers [3], numerous studies have focused on usage of multiple modalities in HCI. Mice equipped with vibrotactile units such as vibration motors and voice coils have been developed to enhance interactions in graphical environments shown on a computer [6]. The iFeelPixel software gives audio and pseudo-tactile feedback during visual-information-centered computer navigation [7]. In earlier work, Lederman et al. emphasized the importance of a haptic grid in discerning data for visual impairments [10]. Kamel et al. designed a grid-based dynamic drawing tool with auditory feedback [9]. For 3D pointing accuracy, Fiorentino et al. concluded that drawing aids such as grids and snaps, which allow users to structure content more easily, are essential for creating a drawing [4]. In the present work, as an extension of these studies, the application of a virtual grid as a working aid in 3-D space is proposed and the grid is implemented using haptic and auditory information.

2 Space Identification Using Multi-modal Information

In this study a 3D work space is divided using a set of virtual grids, which are comprised of non-visual (i.e. haptic and/or auditory) planes. The effectiveness of these augmented haptic and auditory cues is evaluated separately or simultaneously alongside visual pointing information presented in a GUI.

2.1 Subjects

The subjects who participated in the study were six graduate students. They ranged in age from 24 to 27, and all participants had normal hearing. The subjects defined themselves as "right-handed", were free of neuromotor impairment, and reported no known somatosensory disturbances. All of them were naïve as to the purpose and hypotheses of the test, and had little or no prior experience as psychophysical observers.

2.2 Apparatus

Navigation such as point-to-point movement in the 3-D workspace was performed using a SensAble PHANToM Omni®, shown in Fig. 3. The force feedback interface generated was a set of haptic planes in accordance with the experiment modes and current position of the cursor. Sound grid planes are generated through Microsoft's DirectSound API, which can provide sound feedback with low-latency. They were conveyed to users through Sony MDR-NC50 noise canceling headphones.

Fig. 3. PHANTOM® Omni™ for 3-D pointing and haptic grid

2.3 Experiment Setup

2.3.1 Experimental Environment
Fig. 4 shows the 3-D virtual spaces of the left-handed Cartesian coordinate system for the experiments. The red sphere in the figure represents the symbolic cursor and moves in accordance with the subject's hand-movement, which is estimated by the force feedback device. Fig. 4 conceptually shows that the value of the z-axis is increasing.

2.3.2 Stimuli
Haptic and/or sound grid planes are presented to the subjects during exploration of the workspace. Table 1 shows the experiment conditions, i.e., the modalities that are combined to form a virtual grid.

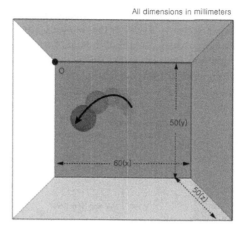

Fig. 4. Schematic of virtual space defined for the experiment

Table 1. Types of modality with respect to grid type

Grid type	Applied Modality
0	-
1	Haptic
2	Auditory
3	Haptic + Auditory

The experimental workspace was set as 60W×50H×50D(mm), a subset of the maximum PHANToM Omni workspace of 160W× 120H×70D (mm), so that all grid planes were parallel along the specific axis and orthogonal to those of the other axes. The experimental space was divided into 150 (=6×5×5) cubic sub-spaces with dimensions of 10mm.

Haptic Grid

The haptic grid is produced and conveyed to subjects via the following steps:

1) When the symbolic cursor of 1mm diameter arrives at a cell borderline, the force feedback device generates a thin plane with 0.25N/mm stiffness.
2) The subject experiences the reaction force, which is perpendicular to the direction of motion and proportional to the applied normal force, according to Hooke's law.
3) If the applied force exceeds 1N, the cursor pops through the grid plane and enters the adjacent cell.

Sound Grid

Sound grids are placed at the same locations as the haptic grids. When navigating in the space of the cell, the subject hears ambient sound at the low frequency of 50Hz (generated at a sampling rate of 22 kHz). As the major frequency components are around the lower limit of human audible frequencies, this ambient sound is barely noticed by the subjects. However, when the cursor moves closer to the grid plane, the frequency (in samples per second) at which the samples are played becomes higher. This transformation, however, does not affect the data format of the audio buffer. The characteristics of the playing frequency that differ from the generated sampling rate are modified using an exponential function that takes the distance from the wall to the cursor as an argument, dx. Fig. 5 illustrates the relation.

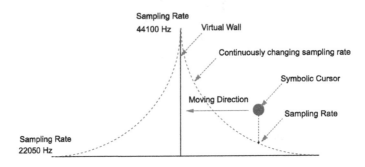

Fig. 5. A sectioned-drawn sound grid: continuously changing playing frequency

The playing sampling rate, i.e., the number of samples played per unit time, dynamically changes according to the distance from the grid wall to the cursor (expressed as dx). The relation is described in the following equation.

$$\text{Playing Sampling Rate(Hz)} = 22050 \times (1 + \exp(-k \times dx)) \tag{1}$$

where the constant term, k, determines the sound-feedback activation area.

When the sound feedback is generated with the haptic feedback simultaneously, as in condition type 3 defined in Table 1, the two modalities are synchronously conveyed. In this study, the frequency of the sound played is updated every 1ms, roughly corresponding to the lowest human auditory threshold [1,2]. All navigation operations are performed using a PHANToM Omni device regardless of the experimental conditions described in Table 1. When the user navigates within the experimental workspace, the cursor is constrained by an outer wall which is rendered visually and, when contact is made, haptically. In this way the user is physically bounded by the workspace. The outer wall's stiffness is 0.5N/mm and the pop-through force is 5N. This feedback informs the user that navigation is not permitted in this vicinity.

2.4 Procedure

During the practice stages of the study, the experimenter described the workspace and the locations of the grid planes to participants. During the test a series of coordinates, which indicated the position of the grid cell (rather than the pixel) to which the subject must navigate were presented. Such a stimulus appeared at the request of the subject and after navigating to the desired cell successfully, the subjects received a visual cue that indicated success.

In each trial of the main experiment, the subjects were asked to move the cursor to pre-defined points, the center of the presented cell, which is described in discreet coordinates. Therefore, the center of each cell is designated as a desired point. The results were recorded in the form of both cell coordinates and actual points, where the latter corresponds with the level of PHANToM Omni's spatial resolution. As Fig. 6 illustrates, the subjects experienced the predefined haptic and sound cues according to the test conditions. Four sets of test conditions were randomly selected for each subject. There are 20 kinds of coordinates; therefore, each subject had to navigate to 80 (=20×4) coordinates in the experiment. During the tests, a specific visual mark was displayed when the cursor was placed at the origin, i.e., the datum point, for correct spatial perception.

Fig. 6. Experimental setup for the space navigation

No visual grid planes were provided during the experiments, as Fig. 7 illustrates. Fig. 7 is an embodiment of Fig. 4, which presents a schematic of the virtual space for the experiment.

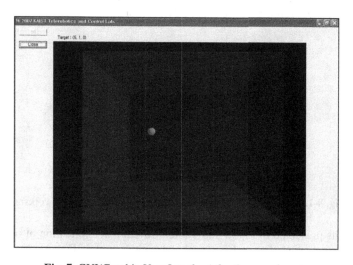

Fig. 7. GUI(Graphic User Interface) for the experiments

2.5 Results

Table 2 presents descriptive statistics providing the Euclidean distance between the desired points and selected points in the 3D workspace. E_TOT refers to the actual Euclidean distance in the 3D space while E_i(i=x,y,z) denotes the distance along the i-axis. The values in the percentage column are the error compared to the no grid condition, i.e. Grid Type = 0.

Table 2. Descriptive statistics of errors

	Grid Type	Mean distance	%	Std. Dev
E_TOT	0	28.28	100.00%	20.87
	1	18.16	64.21%	15.66
	2	17.27	61.06%	12.43
	3	15.72	55.60%	10.61
E_X	0	11.97	100.00%	13.46
	1	9.80	81.85%	11.52
	2	8.92	74.54%	9.55
	3	7.76	64.85%	6.54
E_Y	0	10.78	100.00%	15.64
	1	8.18	75.85%	10.00
	2	7.29	67.63%	6.18
	3	6.94	64.35%	5.56
E_Z	0	18.55	100.00%	14.40
	1	9.66	52.07%	9.30
	2	10.20	55.00%	9.32
	3	9.44	50.90%	9.43

The graphs presented in Fig. 8 provide the mean values of the error versus the grid types. The error bar represents the standard deviation.

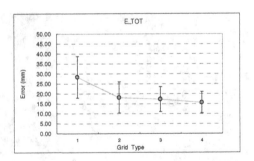

Fig. 8-1. Error between desired point and selected point in 3D workspace

The results presented in Fig. 8 and Table 2 reveal that application of the grid plane in the 3D virtual space diminishes visual ambiguities in the 3D workspace, especially in the z-direction (refer to Fig. 8-4). Therefore, it can be concluded that the existence of the grid plane can enhance the efficiency of performing tasks in 3D space. In the

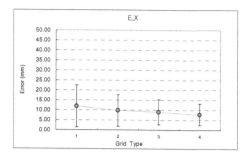

Fig. 8-2. Error between desired point and selected point along the x-axis

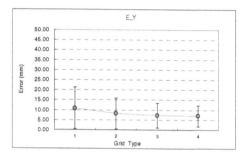

Fig. 8-3. Error between desired point and selected point along the y-axis

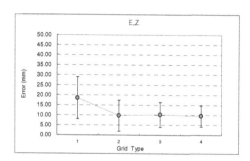

Fig. 8-4. Error between desired point and selected point along the z-axis

statistical tests, a categorical variable, grid type, was chosen as an independent variable and Euclidian error was chosen as a dependent variable. Table 3 shows the statistical results of a one-way ANOVA test.

Table 3. Results from One-Way ANOVA

Grid Type	F	Sig.
0	16.47186	0.00
1	3.393179	0.02
2	3.498236	0.02
3	19.82233	0.00

These statistical results reveal that the depth-ambiguity problem in 3D-space can be significantly reduced by adopted haptic and audio grids (F=19.82, p<0.01). Fig. 9 presents the results of a Tukey's HSD, a post-hoc test for pairwise comparisons performed after one-way ANOVA tests.

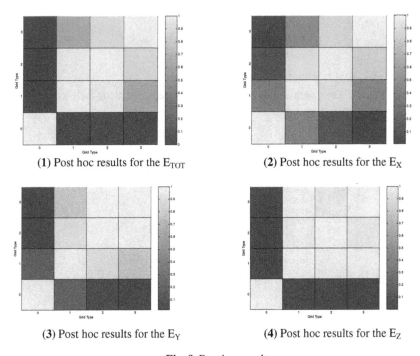

(1) Post hoc results for the E_{TOT} (2) Post hoc results for the E_X

(3) Post hoc results for the E_Y (4) Post hoc results for the E_Z

Fig. 9. Post hoc results

A post-hoc test is needed after completing an ANOVA in order to determine which groups differ from each other. For reference, in the graphs of Fig. 9, as the number becomes smaller (represented by redder colors, as described in the vertical color scale), the difference between pairs becomes more significant. The results show that the deviation along the z-direction is diminished by the addition of the grid planes. It was also found that simultaneous presentation of haptic and auditory planes is the most effective approach for accurate navigation.

2.6 Discussion of the Results

The graphs presented in Fig. 10 show the actual coordinates used during the experiments. For readability, only half of the total data is presented. Because exploration strategies of the subjects are inherently different, the following graphs comparing the trajectories according to the applied modalities depict the data of one randomly chosen subject. The transition of color from blue to violet represents the time sequence. These figures show that the trajectories generally converge to one particular point, that is, the origin located at the left-topmost corner. We speculate that this origin point plays a role as a datum position. This may provide accurate spatial awareness to the users. Also, it can be observed that if there are physical grid planes that divide the workspace, the user tends to tangentially follow these planes. This allows users to perform more efficient navigation in 3D space, which may accompany the visual ambiguities revealed by the visual results. When no physical grid is provided, the user engages in many hovering actions (Fig. 10-1).

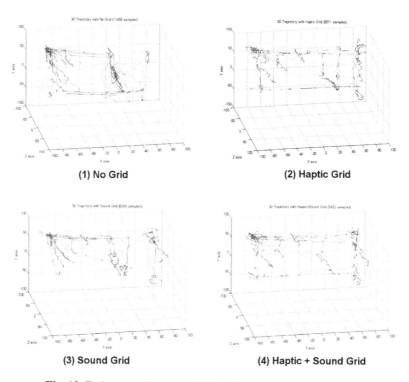

Fig. 10. Trajectory of one user (WH) with respect to grid condition

3 Conclusion

In this study and compared to a condition without grids, error was decreased to 64.85% in the x-axis, 64.35% in the y-axis, and 50.90% in the z-axis when physical grid planes are provided during 3D navigation. The information most enhanced by the presence of the grid were the depth cues along the z-axis, as Table 2 shows. Because the information concerning the x- and y- direction is visually provided to the users, errors in the x-y (2D) plane were inherently not as large as those in the z-direction, even when no grid is provided. Previously, Fritz et al. also reported that a haptic grid was necessary to approximate location when visual information is not fully available [5]. We can conclude that grid type 3, which consists of both haptic and sound modalities, is the most effective in terms of reducing errors in the 3D space. As the haptic and sound grids were found to enhance task performance accuracy in 3D navigation, they can be utilized as a working aid in tasks such as 3D modeling, games, or other works that require precise user spatial awareness.

4 General Discussion

Combining visual, auditory, and haptic feedback is important in multimodal human computer interaction (MMHCI). For MMHCI, we have augmented haptic and auditory feedback. Fig. 11 [8] illustrates the importance of multimodal feedback in implementing a human-centered interface.

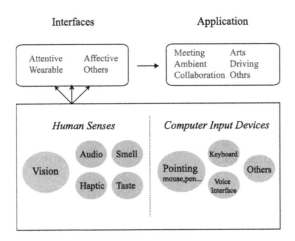

Fig. 11. Overview of multimodal interaction [8]

As further work, we intend to use different grid configurations, such as major grids divided into several minor grids in the same workspace, similar to real-world rulers and comprised of various modalities. By employing grids which feature different sensations in the same workspace it may be possible to provide more accurate spatial awareness to users something that may prove useful in any task involving navigating in virtual spaces.

Acknowledgement

This research has been supported by 'Smart Haptic Interface Project (2006-S-031, Korea Ministry of Information and Communication)' and 'Development of Immersive Tangible Experience Space Technology (KIST)'.

References

[1] Eddins, D.A., Green, D.M.: Temporal integration and temporal resolution, Hearing. Handbook of perception and cognition (1995)
[2] Efron, R.: Conservation of temporal information by perceptual systems. Perception and Psychophysics 14, 518–553O (1973)
[3] Ellis, S.R.: What are virtual environments? Computer Graphics and Applications 14(1), 17–22 (1994)

[4] Fiorentino, M., Monno, G., Renzulli, P.A., Uva, A.E.: 3D Pointing in Virtual Reality: Experimental Study (2003)

[5] Fritz, J.P., Way, T.P., Barner, K.E.: Haptic representation of scientific data for visually impaired or blind persons (1996)

[6] Hughes, R.G., Forrest, A.R.: Perceptualisation using a tactile mouse. In: Visualization 1996. Proceedings, pp. 181–188 (1996)

[7] iFeelPixel™ (2006), http://www.ifeelpixel.com/

[8] Jaimes, A., Sebe, N.: Multimodal Human Computer Interaction: A Survey. Computer Vision and Image (2006)

[9] Kamel, H.M., Landay, J.A.: Sketching images eyes-free: a grid-based dynamic drawing tool for the blind, pp. 33–40. ACM Press, New York (2002)

[10] Lederman, S.J., Campbell, J.I.: Tangible graphs for the blind. Hum Factors 24(1), 85–100 (1982)

User-Centered Design Proposals for Prototyping Haptic User Interfaces

Hans V. Bjelland and Kristian Tangeland

Department of Product Design, Norwegian University of Science and Technology,
7491 Trondheim, Norway
hans.bjelland@ntnu.no, tangelan@stud.ntnu.no

Abstract. The range of applications for haptic user interfaces is wide, but although haptics offer unique qualities to user interfaces, the rate of adoption and implementation of haptics in commercialized products is relatively low. The challenges of building low-cost flexible prototypes with haptics in the early stages of product development are believed to be a contributing factor to this. This paper addresses these specific challenges in relation to the user-centered design process. A case where prototypes were used in the early project stage is presented as an example of possibilities of prototyping haptic feedback. Finally, general recommendations for how to prototype haptic user interfaces that support both technological development and usability are listed. These are comprised by: 1) Build on the tradition of user-centered design, 2) Prototype from day one, 3) Substitute technology, 4) Build several different prototypes, 5) Develop a vocabulary, 6) Stick with the heuristics. These recommendations can contribute to a better understanding of how haptics can be handled in the design process as well as guide future haptic research.

Keywords: prototyping, haptic user interfaces, user-centered design.

1 Introduction

A haptic user interface is an interface where the user interacts through the sense of touch by providing haptic feedback and/or sensing body movement. The complexity of a haptic user interface varies significantly, ranging from devices with passive haptic displays or simple vibrotactile haptic feedback, to complex systems with dynamic haptic feedback and sensing of finger, hand, head or body movement. The range of applications of haptic user interfaces is wide, spanning from the medical and aviation industry to gaming and virtual reality, but although haptics offer unique qualities to user interfaces, the rate of adoption and implementation of haptics in commercialized products is low. Research on haptics has until recently been dominated by how to solve the technical challenges of this technology, mainly using high-tech solutions.

As the technology matures we need to address how haptics can be handled in the design process. MacLean promotes using a "top-down" approach when designing an interface that utilize haptics, starting with the user needs – "to provide an effective interface to a given application" – and find solutions built on available technologies

I. Oakley and S. Brewster (Eds.): HAID 2007, LNCS 4813, pp. 110–120, 2007.

and methods [1]. However, much of the research carried out in the field of haptics focus on the technological development and studies how users respond to it in laboratory experiments with highly controlled parameters. This focus is therefore more of a "bottom-up" approach. This is necessary from a technological point of view and can provide important insights about specific usability issues, but will not necessarily lead directly to successful commercialized products.

Prototypes are central in both the development of new ideas and concepts, and in including users in the design process to ensure usability. We believe that the difficult task of building low-cost prototypes that include haptic user interfaces during the early stages of an product development processes is an important reason for the low implementation rate. Before a broad commercialization of haptic user interfaces, it is important to gain better knowledge of prototyping to develop the best products and to intensify the work on usability within the field of haptics.

The ISO 13407 [2] standard defines a prototype as: "representation of all or part of a product or system that, although limited in some way, can be used for evaluation". Prototypes built in the early stages of product development are usually restricted by limited availability of time and resources [3], leading to simplified prototypes, lacking functionality and complexity that will be present in the final product. Still, they should answer important questions about the concept and form a basis for the development of product requirements. The interaction with haptic user interfaces is greatly dependent on the subtle nuances of its haptic properties. This represents a major challenge when prototyping. Hence the research question of this paper:

How can we prototype product concepts that utilize haptics, within the limitations of an early product development phase, and still gain the necessary insight needed from the prototype?

Addressing these issues by looking at haptic technologies in general, offers some obvious challenges, as haptic devices are very diverse. There are, however, some significant similarities between the different technologies in regard to the haptic modality and the devices' physical attributes that makes such a broad focus valuable. We believe that integrating the perspectives of user-centered design and haptics is beneficial, not only to product developers, but also to guide future haptic research.

In section 2 of this paper the use of prototyping in the user-centered product development process is addressed and various characteristics of different types of prototypes are described. In section 3 a case study describing the development of throttle sticks with haptic feedback is presented. Recommendations for prototyping of haptic user interfaces are given in Section 4.

2 Prototyping

Prototyping during early stages of product development is an important step to reduce development time by early verification, visualization and communication of product concepts. Better communication inside of the project group and more relevant feedback from users due to the use of prototypes will lower the project risk significantly and increase the usability of the final product [4].

2.1 Prototypes in User-Centered Design

Prototyping plays a central role in both heuristic evaluation and usability testing of product concepts, which are key factors in a user-centered design process [4] and human factors and ergonomics engineering in general. Not only does it represent the methods and techniques required to design usable products and systems, but also the philosophy of placing the user in the center of the process [5].

Heuristic evaluation, or expert evaluation, of a design means analytically considering the characteristics of a product or system against human factors criteria. This should be carried out by several individuals in order to detect key problems [4]. Heuristic evaluation enables an increased number of iterations during the user-centered design process, since it does not involve time consuming testing with real users. Thus, more ideas and concepts can be evaluated, resulting in a better product.

Usability testing is deployed to determine the usability of a product, taking into account the user, the user's goals and use context. Testing can be based on varying methods, in many phases of the product development process, to give valuable feedback and confirm that requirements are met.

Iterations during the user-centered design process, constantly refining and optimizing the concept, are important to achieve usability in the final product and minimizing the risk of not meeting requirements [1]. Vicente [6] proposes a model for human factors research, based on an iterative process, where the type of user testing varies between highly controlled laboratory experiments and qualitative, descriptive field studies, in order to gain representative knowledge about the final product. This implies developing several different prototypes that can be used in the various types of user tests to obtain a sufficient overall understanding of the usability aspects.

2.2 Types of Prototypes

Schrage [7] stresses that managing a diversified prototype portfolio plays a key role in developing innovative concepts, avoiding flaws due to specific qualities of one prototyping medium and covering all the various aspects of the final product regarding both technical functionality and usability. Prototypes can have varying characteristics, and these can vary along different axes:

- Physical ↔ Virtual
- Low-Fidelity ↔ High Fidelity
- Vertical ↔ Horizontal
- Exploratory ↔ Experimental
- Low user involvement ↔ High user involvement

Prototypes can be physical, virtual or a combination of the two. Computer assisted design (CAD) have become a helpful tool during product development, and can increase the number of iterations possible within a limited time frame [7]. Rapid prototyping technologies allow for a repeated transition between a virtual and materialized prototype. Another way to touch virtual prototypes is through specific haptic user interfaces like the PHANTOM™.

The fidelity of a prototype is a measurement of how well it simulates its representing real-world system [8]. Low-fidelity prototypes represent a reduction in functionality and number of features and have relatively low cost. They are often used in the early phases of product development to rapidly test general principles and reduce the level of uncertainty [7]. Schrage [7] argues that "rapid prototyping means rapid failures", which imply that by using low-fidelity prototypes, principal errors in both technical functionality and usability can be discovered at an early stage, thus lowering the project risk. Low-fidelity prototypes are used in most fields and can be made out of almost any material that suits the purpose, from cardboard and wood to nails and rubber bands.

On the other hand, high-fidelity prototypes have a high degree of features and functionality, and are often used in later stages of product development. The costs might be high for such a prototype, but it can give more detailed information about the concept, and therefore play an important role in this latter stage of product development.

A prototype can be vertical or horizontal [9]. In a vertical prototype some features are cut away while others are fully implemented. This can be used for both proof of technological concept for parts of the system as well as for user testing of certain elements. A horizontal prototype includes all features, but has reduced functionality. This can be useful in order to test usability aspects of the whole system before the technology has been developed.

Depending on the intended use of a prototype, it can be described as exploratory or experimental. An exploratory prototype is used to investigate alternative designs, identify requirements and clarify project goals. An experimental prototype is used to validate system specifications [10]. The degree of user involvement is also a way to characterize prototypes. When testing exploratory prototypes, user involvement is normally high.

2.3 Prototyping Haptic Feedback

There are many specific challenges related to prototyping haptic feedback. As earlier stated interaction with haptic user interfaces is greatly dependent on the subtle nuances of its haptic properties. In early stages of product development there is a need for tools that can provide a flexible and efficient platform to explore possible solutions that have satisfying haptic qualities. Some prototyping platforms exist, both as hardware, software and combined kits. Little is, however, known about how the user experience of such platforms qualitatively or quantitatively can be compared to the user experience of a final technical implementation. Similarly, little is known about how such platforms can be incorporated into the early stages of product development.

3   Case Study – Throttle Sticks

We will present a case study where exploratory prototypes were utilized in the early project stages to quickly establish a proof of concept. The presentation of the case study will be limited to the scope of this paper.

3.1   Case Background

High Speed Crafts (HSC) is a class of ships that have top speeds of minimum 25 knots, and have a lightweight construction. Their characteristic features are the combination of high speeds and their operation in closed waters. On early HSCs the throttle sticks often controlled the thrust of the engines through a mechanical air valve transmission directly. Along with the general digitalization and automation of the maritime transport this system is mostly replaced by automated motor controls and electronic throttle sticks (Fig. 1).

Fig. 1. Electronic throttle sticks used in various high speed crafts

There are obvious advantages with an automated motor control, such as liberating the navigator from the throttle sticks during acceleration and prolonged engine life due to gentle acceleration and retardation. However, as we elsewhere have discussed, such a change in the control system alters basic qualities of the throttle sticks with respect to handling and haptic properties [11]. The control is generally less direct and lacks the perceptual richness present in the old systems in a way that gives the navigator less information about the control situation.

Based on the challenges of the new throttle sticks we initiated a project to explore the possibilities of utilizing haptics to improve the throttle sticks. We did not intend to recreate the touch and feel of the old interface, as the overall system also has changed, but wanted the throttle sticks to supply the navigator with more information about the state of the system.

The interaction with the throttle sticks takes part in a complex task of navigation, involving a range of different technical equipment and social interaction with other crew members. These are important considerations in the development of new throttle stick solutions. The description of the project will, however, in this paper be limited to the experiences gained from using prototypes in the early development process.

3.2 Prototype Development

In the early development process it was important to explore different possibilities and develop proofs of concept to form a basis for further development. As the initial ideas about utilizing haptics were ill-defined there was a need to be able to quickly develop and evaluate different concepts through prototypes. This was an open ended preliminary exploration and the tools used to prototype needed to be both flexible and affordable, as time and resources was limited.

Because of previous experience and availability modified computer peripherals became a valuable resource in our prototype development. Gaming equipment, such as force feedback wheels and vibrotactile computer mice that can be purchased off the shelf, connect to a computer and offers standard APIs to communicate and program, like the DirectX on the Windows™ platform.

The first prototype was based on a Logitech® Formula™ Force Wheel. The wheel was substituted with a stick and positioned in a way that made its geometry comparable to that of the electronic throttle sticks. The prototype was connected to a computer and controlled through a program interface. The various force feedback effects were programmed in Immersion Studio®. Macromedia Flash® 8 was used to relate these effects to the spatial position of the stick and to explore the use of many simultaneous effects.

The first prototype confirmed the potential of the prototype setup and initiated new ideas. The motor in the force feedback wheel was well suited to give a notion of friction and spring forces. It was, however, less suitable to give subtle vibrotactile signals.

To provide the desired vibrotactile signals a modified Logitech® IFeel™ Mouseman was implemented in the second prototype setup as a second source of feedback (Fig. 2). The program interface was modified to incorporate both peripherals.

The control situation of the throttle sticks is affected by many parameters. The four most significant parameters identified was the physical position of the sticks, the rate of change to this position, the engine speed and the difference between the engine speed and the position of the throttles. These were graphically represented in the programming interface as horizontal axes that could trigger various haptic feedback (Fig. 3). This made it possible to rapidly explore different concepts.

Fig. 2. The wheel was substituted with a stick and controlled by the computer. In the second prototype a modified vibrotactile mouse was used to give the desired vibrotactile signals.

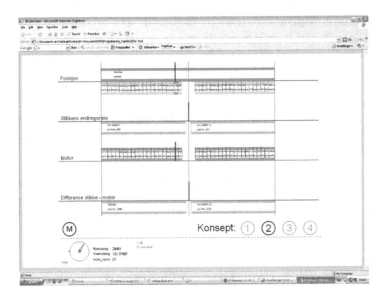

Fig. 3. The programming interface shows the activation of forces in real time

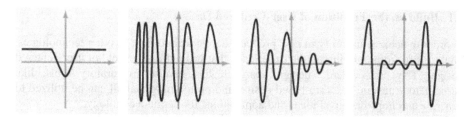

Fig. 4. Graphical representations of haptic effects used during the project

In addition to the graphical programming interface various graphical representations of haptic effects were developed to assist the development process (Fig. 4). This made it easier to visualize ideas and to discuss different concepts.

3.3 Case Results

Through exploratory prototypes based on highly available computer accessories it was possible to create prototypes that had a reasonably high fidelity that adequately corresponded to the stages of idea development. The haptic properties of the resulting prototypes were nearly comparable to what to expect from a finished product. This prototype worked as a proof of concept and was well suited to base decisions regarding the future work on the system.

The use of prototypes made it possible to get immediate feedback on design changes throughout these early development stages. It made it easy to test out new ideas and bad ideas could quickly be eliminated. The various graphical representations helped the development team to maintain a reference and common vocabulary.

4 Recommendations for Prototyping of Haptic User Interfaces

When prototyping haptic user interfaces, it is important to address both the unique qualities of the haptic sense and the role prototypes play in the product development process as a means of communication and a way to test concepts. Most documented development projects where haptic user interfaces have been implemented are research based, and they have been focused on exploring specific technological or user aspects. The research is rarely part of a commercial product development process. Thus, there exist little documentation on the relationship between prototype and commercialized product. Still, based on the two previous sections, some recommendations for prototyping of haptic user interfaces will be suggested. They have a particular relevance during early product development phases where time and cost limitations are most crucial.

The recommendations are general, which reflect the lack of more specific experience and research. They can, in addition to guide product developers, serve as a base for further discussion about future focus areas for the haptics research community.

4.1 Build on the Tradition of User-Centered Design

In order to achieve usability in new products haptic technology, as other technologies, might profit from building on the experience that lies within the field of user-centered design. The user-centered design approach has several exploratory tools, like participatory design, scenario-based design and prototyping that all can be utilized to generate and improve novel ideas and applications for haptic technology.

Due to the complex nature of interaction through several senses, prototyping as a central part of user-centered design should be prioritized and explored extensively. By conducting both laboratory experiments and qualitative field studies, based on prototypes with various characteristics, the gained knowledge as a whole will probably support a better understanding of the complex interaction.

4.2 Prototype from Day One

Early exploration of ideas and concepts will speed up the process by generating more ideas and reveal hidden errors [7]. By utilizing the cost and time saving qualities of lower fidelity prototypes, imitations of an interface's haptic properties can be explored during earlier phases of product development. It is evident that prototypes of haptic user interfaces require a certain degree of technological complexity during later stages of development, but developers should strive to prototype fast and simple in the beginning. This might ultimately lead to a faster release of a better product to a lower cost. The challenges of prototyping on alternative devices or technologies are discussed below.

4.3 Substitute Technology

Due to the nuance and high resolution of the haptic sense, it is difficult to fake a haptic user interface in a low-fidelity prototype. A way to avoid this is by substituting the haptic properties with another technology or already existing product. Analog, mechanical devices can be used, as well as modifications of existing products. In addition, some haptic user interface developer kits can be purchased off the shelf that allow for quick implementation of haptics in user interfaces.

In the case study presented above both a force feedback wheel and vibrotactile computer mouse was combined to refine the haptic feedback in the prototype. Still, it is difficult to fully predict how the user experience of a prototype that makes use of an alternative device or technology will compare to that of a final system. More studies are therefore needed to better understand how the variability between the haptic devices could be managed in development projects.

Shortcomings in each individual prototyping medium can partly be met by utilizing several different prototypes, as discussed below.

4.4 Build Several Different Prototypes

As Schrage [7] stresses, several different prototypes should be built using varying prototyping medium, to encourage interplay and dialogue between the various representations. Interplay between physical and virtual models, or in between different physical or virtual models has proven useful within different industries [7] and might be beneficial for haptic user interfaces when solving technological challenges and assuring usability.

Another way of diversification is by developing both vertical and horizontal prototypes. By using both types, detailed knowledge about some aspects can be investigated, without loosing overview [9]. This is particularly important in complex use environments.

Certain aspects of a design solution will not be represented by a prototype, with possible consequences for the generalization and relevance of a user-test to certain product features [3]. By developing prototypes with different characteristics made from varying modeling medium, estimations and lack of realism might be better taken into account during evaluation, both for work within the project group and in relation to user tests. This might be a relevant method to increase the validity of the evaluation.

4.5 Develop a Vocabulary

It is important to establish a vocabulary to describe the haptic properties of a prototype during evaluation. Such verbalization is particularly important during transition between succeeding prototypes to preserve acquired knowledge and during user tests if interactions should be explained by the test person [3]. Various project specific vocabularies have been developed and used to classify and rate variations of haptic feedback [12, 13]. These might in addition to technical, physical or graphical analogies be useful when developing an adequate vocabulary for a specific project.

The haptics research community could greatly ease the use of effective vocabularies in product development projects by developing more general vocabularies that are adapted to the needs of a user-centered design process.

4.6 Stick with the Heuristics

Heuristics are important when evaluating prototypes of user interfaces. They let designers make evaluations and decisions without a need for full insight into a particular field of research. As an example of how heuristics can be developed to support future product development van Erp presents recommendations regarding the properties of vibrotactile displays in HCI [14]. There are, however, few existing heuristics for haptic user interfaces. As the characteristics of haptic user interfaces vary greatly, chances are small that there are any heuristics available for a particular haptic application. By focusing on developing heuristics and by letting the technology mature more heuristics can be made available to the designers.

5 Conclusion

Haptics can ad unique qualities to an interface. Today, the sense of touch is being introduced and even reintroduced as a means of interaction in products, but to what extent this actually improves the usability varies significantly. The development is mostly technologically driven, with a focus on what can be done instead of what should be done from a user's point of view. In order to utilize haptic technologies to create a simpler, more humane interaction, a stronger focus should be put on user-centered design. In this paper some recommendations for how haptic user interfaces could be prototyped as part of a user-centered design process are suggested. With the specific qualities of the haptic sense in mind, both its possibilities and challenges, the potential of prototyping has been explored.

Future research is necessary within all the recommended focus areas to better understand how prototypes of haptic user interfaces could be utilized. This should be carried out to support the development of a more detailed design methodology, with a foundation in the tradition of user-centered design.

References

1. MacLean, K.E.: Designing with Haptic Feedback. In: ICRA 2000. Symposium on Haptic Feedback in the Proc. of IEEE Robotics and Automation, San Francisco, USA, pp. 22–28. IEEE Computer Society Press, Los Alamitos (2000)
2. ISO 13407: Human-centered design processes for interactive systems (1999)
3. Rooden, M.J.: Prototypes on Trial. In: Green, W.S., Jordan, P.W. (eds.) Human Factors in Product Design: Current Practice and Future Trends, pp. 138–150. Taylor & Francis, London (2001)
4. Wickens, C.D., Lee, J.D., Liu, Y., Gordon Becker, S.E.: An Introduction to Human Factors Engineering. Prentice-Hall, Englewood Cliffs (2004)
5. Vavik, T., Øritsland, T.A.: Mennesklige aspekter i design.Tapir Uttrykk, NTNU, Norway (1999)
6. Vicente, K.J.: Heeding the Legacy of Meister, Brunswik, & Gibson: Toward a Broader View of Human Factors Research. Human Factors 39(2), 323–328 (1997)
7. Schrage, M.: Serious Play. Harvard Business School Press, Boston (1999)
8. Schricker, B.C., Franceschini, R.W., Johnson, T.C.: Fidelity Evaluation Framework. In: Proc. 34th Simulation Symposium, 116th edn., Seattle, WA, April 22-26, pp. 109–116 (2001)
9. Nielsen, J.: Usability Engineering. Academic Press, Inc (1993)
10. Maner, W.: Prototyping. Online document cited 2006 October 15, March 15 (1997), Available http://web.cs.bgsu.edu/maner/domains/Proto.htm
11. Bjelland, H.V., Roed, B.K., Hoff, T.: Studies on throttle sticks in high speed crafts – haptics in mechanical, electronic and haptic feedback interfaces. In: Proc. of the First Joint Eurohaptics Conference and Symposium on Haptic Interfaces for Virtual Environment and Teleoperator Systems 2005, pp. 509–510. IEEE Computer Society Press, Los Alamitos (2005)
12. van Erp, J.B.F., Spapé, M.M.A.: Distilling the Underlying Dimensions of Tactile Melodies. In: Proc. of Eurohaptics 2003., Dublin, Ireland, July 6-9, pp. 111–120 (2003)
13. Schütte, S., Eklund, J.: Design of rocker switches for work-vehicles: an application of Kansei Engineering. Applied Ergonomics 36(5), 557–567 (2005)
14. van Erp, J.B.F.: Guidelines for the use of vibro-tactile displays in Human computer interaction. In: Proc. of Eurohaptics 2002, University of Edinburgh, Scotland, University of Edinburgh, Scotland, pp. 18–22 (2002)

Designing Eyes-Free Interaction

Ian Oakley and Jun-Seok Park

POST-PC Research Group, Electronics and Telecommunication Research Institute
161 Gajeong-dong, Yuseong-gu, Daejeon, 305-700, Republic of Korea
{ian,parkjs}@etri.re.kr

Abstract. As the form factors of computational devices diversify, the concept of eyes-free interaction is becoming increasingly relevant: it is no longer hard to imagine use scenarios in which screens are inappropriate. However, there is currently little consensus about this term. It is regularly employed in different contexts and with different intents. One key consequence of this multiplicity of meanings is a lack of easily accessible insights into how to best build an eyes-free system. This paper seeks to address this issue by thoroughly reviewing the literature, proposing a concise definition and presenting a set of design principles. The application of these principles is then elaborated through a case study of the design of an eyes-free motion input system for a wearable device.

Keywords: Eyes-free interaction, design principles, motion input.

1 Introduction

Modern user interfaces come in a vast range of shapes and sizes, an inevitable consequence of the spread of complex computational functionality from the office computers where it first evolved to the living rooms, cars, sofas, pockets and even clothes of everyday users. The rich graphical interaction paradigm developed for desktop personal computers is clearly inappropriate for an ultra-portable music player intended for joggers, and arguably a poor fit for even a sophisticated smart phone [13]. Indeed, there is a growing realization that the design of an interface needs to be tightly coupled to the context in which it is intended to be used, and an acknowledgement that the range of use contexts is growing rapidly wider.

This paper seeks to define, review, and explore the literature on one such class of new interface, termed eyes-free. This terminology has been in use for several decades as a descriptive phrase denoting a UI with little or no graphical component, but we argue that it is now emerging as a specialized interaction design area in and of itself, with unique features and qualities. Historically, the literature that has employed this term is distinctly heterogeneous: it originates from divergent motivations, addresses different domains, adopts different interaction paradigms and leverages different modalities. Authors have tacitly acknowledged this lack of accord by treating the term cautiously (typically using it italicized or wrapped in quotations). In this way, no unifying consensus has emerged regarding what exactly makes an interface eyes-free and, more importantly, what qualities makes one effective. Creating an interface that

I. Oakley and S. Brewster (Eds.): HAID 2007, LNCS 4813, pp. 121–132, 2007.
© Springer-Verlag Berlin Heidelberg 2007

operates effectively without vision is a challenging task, but there are currently few general-purpose and easily accessible insights into how this might be achieved.

By offering a thorough review of the eyes-free literature, drawing out the themes that underlie it, this paper hopes to dispel the confusion surrounding this term and offer a set of principles against which future eyes-free system designers can position their work and understand the options available to them and the issues they will face. Less formal than a full theoretical explanation, this kind of framework has been widely applied in the HCI literature to systemize the design process, providing a focus and common language to facilitate discussions [18]. The review commences with an overview of the use of the term eyes-free in the HCI literature in order to delineate the scope of the research considered here. It then moves on to discuss the motivations that underlie the development of eyes-free systems and the properties of the different input and output modalities that have been employed to produce them. It culminates with a working definition and a set of principles for the design of eyes-free interfaces. This paper concludes by describing the design of an eyes-free interface for a wearable computing system which illustrates how these principles might be applied.

2 Eyes-Free Literature Review

2.1 History, Domains and Scope

Three domains which regularly reference the term eyes-free are voice recognition, gesture recognition and access technologies for the visually impaired. In the first, it is often coupled with the term hands-free and serves to describe two of the key features of voice input technology: it requires no mouse and no screen. In the second, it alludes to the fact that once learnt, users can perform gestures in the absence of graphical feedback; indeed as most systems do not feature any interactive feedback on the state of gestures, eyes-free use is the default mode. In both these domains, research tends to focus on improving recognition algorithms or the development, refinement and pedagogy of the semantically rich commands sets they support. In this way, we argue that the term eyes-free is peripheral, rather than central, to these research areas, and exclude them from the mandate of this paper. We make a similar distinction with access technologies for visually impaired users. The term eyes-free is an appropriate adjective, but the focus of this research area substantially differs from that which considers the wider population. An article from the former might focus on mathematical visualization techniques, while one from the latter, the interface to a personal music player. This paper is interested in this latter approach, and so excludes work conducted under the more established banner of access technologies.

Eyes free-interaction has been approached as an extension of work to reduce the amount of screen real estate taken up by a UI. With its roots in efforts to shrink graphical user interfaces through the presentation of audio or haptic feedback, this research has tended to focus on creating non-visual versions of user interface elements such as progress bars [4]. One important trend within this work is that it tends to focus on notification events, such as the completion of a file download or page load in a web browser page [16]. The simplicity of this scenario (where a single sporadically delivered bit of information may be sufficient) places light demands on the level and quantity of interaction required.

Work on audio (and less commonly haptic [17]) visualization has also used the term eyes-free, referring to the fact that the state of some system can be monitored without visual attention. Representative audio visualization work includes Gaver's [6] classic study of collaborative control of machines in a virtual factory and applied studies such as Watson and Sanderson's evaluations of structured sounds from a pulse monitor in a hospital scenario [21]. Finally, the term-eyes free is now also appearing in domains such as mobile [11], wearable [1], and pervasive computing. The typical approach in these systems is the design of a new input technique which enables interaction without visual attention. In particular it is this design process, in these emerging and demanding domains, that this paper seeks to shed light on.

2.2 Motivations

The fundamental motivation for eyes-free interaction is that as it leaves visual attention unoccupied, users are free to perform additional tasks [1], [17], [27]. Authors cite this motivation both in contexts where users are expected to be engaged in tasks in the real world (walking, driving) and tasks on their device (talking, typing). Underlying this proposition is the assumption that the cognitive resources consumed by the eyes-free interface will be sufficiently modest as to enable this. Essentially, an eyes-free interface is one that need operate not only without vision, but also without consuming an appreciable amount of thought or attention. An audio or haptic interface which requires focus to operate is unlikely to support even trivial multi-tasking. This places an additional challenge to eyes-free interface design that is arguably as central and demanding as the exclusion of visual cues.

The majority of other motivations are domain focused. Researchers in mobile interaction highlight the problems with screens on handheld devices: they consume power (reducing battery life), can be hard to see in bright conditions and it may simply be inconvenient to fetch the device from wherever it is kept just to look at its screen [27]. There is also a trend for mobile devices to feature larger screens and fewer buttons. One of the key ergonomic properties of buttons is that they can be identified and operated by touch alone, and the fact they are diminishing in numbers is likely to raise the importance of alternative forms of eyes-free interaction [11]. These same issues tend to be exacerbated in wearable computing scenarios, where researchers have also highlighted the inherent mobility and privacy [5] of interacting without looking as motivating factors for their systems.

2.3 Input Modalities

Eyes-free input is characterized by simple gestural interactions which can be classified by conditional logic. Researchers have studied movements of styli [8], the finger [13], the hand [11], head [1] and even purely muscular gestures [5]. In each case, the movements themselves are closely coupled to the constraints of chosen bodily part. For example, marking menus [8], a well studied stylus based interaction technique, typically features straight strokes in all four cardinal directions as these can be performed (and distinguished) easily, comfortably and rapidly. In contrast, when studying head gestures, Brewster *et al.* [1] proposed a system that relied on turning of the head to highlight specific items and nods forward to select them. Nods backwards were not included as they were found to cause some discomfort and awkwardness. Similarly Zhao *et al.* [27] studied circular motions of the thumb against a handheld touchpad, as these fall within a comfortable and discrete range of motion.

A second common characteristic of eyes-free input is that it involves movements which are kinesthetically identifiable. The stylus strokes, turns and nods of the head or translations of the thumb mentioned above can all be monitored by users through their awareness of the state of their own body. It is trivial to distinguish between stroking downwards with a pen and stroking upwards. Equally, we are kinesthetically, albeit usually sub-consciously, aware of the orientations of our head with respect to our body at all times. The kinesthetic sense is often cited as the only bi-directional sense, in which motor output (in the form of some movement, muscular tension or strain) is tightly coupled to sensory input from the muscles, joints and skin informing us about this activity [20]. Taking advantage of this closed feedback loop is an implicit but important aspect of an eyes-free interface.

Although, as described in the next section, eyes-free interfaces are typically supported by explicitly generated audio or haptic cues, we argue that these messages are used to reinforce and augment the fundamental and inherent kinesthetic awareness that underpins eyes-free interaction. Kinesthetic input is the key factor that enables an eyes-free system to be operated fluidly and with confidence; explicitly generated additional cues add semantic content and beneficial redundancy to this basic property.

2.4 Output Modalities

Eyes-free feedback has appeared as audio icons (semantically meaningful sampled sounds) [1], earcons (structured audio messages composed of variations in the fundamental properties of sounds such pitch and rhythm) [4] and speech [27]. In some cases the audio is also spatialized. Haptic systems have used both tactile [11] and force-feedback [17] output. These output channels vary considerably as to the richness of the feedback they support. For example, all three forms of audio output can arguably convey richer semantic content than haptic feedback, and of these, speech more than either audio icons or earcons. However, several other qualities influence the suitability of output modalities to eyes-free interaction.

The speed with which information can be displayed and absorbed is an important quality for an eyes-free interface. For example, a system based on user input, followed by several seconds attending to spoken output message, followed by additional input is unlikely to yield a rapid, satisfying or low workload experience. Indeed, such a paradigm, in the form of the automatic telephone menu systems commonly adopted by the call-centers of large companies, is widely acknowledged to be both frustrating and laborious [26]. This issue is exacerbated by the fact that a common eyes-free design technique is to segment some input space into discrete targets and provide feedback on transitions between these. Such transitions are usually designed to take place extremely rapidly; similarly immediate feedback is required to support them. This constraint can be satisfied at the cost of sacrificing the amount of information transferred in each message; a short cue signifying that an event has occurred is simply crafted, but it is considerably more difficult to convey an easily understood description of a command. The multi-dimensional trade off between the amount of information contained within user interface feedback, the speed with which this can be achieved and the amount of effort and attention required to interpret it is especially important in the eyes-free domain.

Eyes-free interfaces have also relied on continually (or ambiently) displayed background information. Inspired by every-day occurrences such as monitoring the performance of car's engine through the variations in its sound, this paradigm is arguably best suited to non-speech audio interfaces, and in particular to tasks which involve casually observing background events as opposed to issuing commands. It has a history in sonification [6], [21] where it has been shown that it can be informative, unobtrusive and effective.

The choice of feedback modality for eyes-free output is also mediated by the characteristics of the domain considered. Audio output is ideal for controlling a personal music player, where the clear perception of sounds through headphones is almost guaranteed. Its suitability may be in more doubt in other situations, where feedback from a device might be obscured by ambient noise or, alternatively, disturb other users. Equally, the use of tactile cues requires users to wear or hold an actuator of some sort and recent research has suggested [10] that perceptual abilities may be impaired when users are engaged in other tasks. It is also worth noting that some events may not require explicit feedback; the changes to the system state may be sufficient to indicate the action has taken place. Representative examples include actions such as terminating an alarm or answering an incoming call.

2.5 Learning Issues

One significant issue for eyes-free interfaces is how they are explored and learnt by a novice user. One reason for the considerable success of current graphical interfaces is that they support an exploratory mode of learning in which functionality can be explored and discovered – buttons can be clicked, menus scanned and mistakes undone from the offset. Given the constraints on the amount of information that can be displayed in an eyes-free interface, achieving a similar flexibility can be a challenge. The basic approach to solving this problem has been to introduce feedback which naturally scales; a novice can attend to it in detail, while an expert can ignore or skip over it. The concept is rooted in marking menus [8]. Typically, these systems feature four item graphical pie menus which users operate by making stylus strokes in cardinal directions. A typical example might involve tapping the screen to summon the menu, followed by visually scanning the items to identify an edit command at the base. Stroking downwards invokes the relevant sub-menu, in which a copy command is displayed on the right. It can then be selected by a rightwards motion. Through nothing more than repeated operation, users become able to dispense with the graphical feedback and simply draw an L shape when they wish to issue a copy command.

Zhao *et al.* [27] present a system which applies this concept to the speech output domain. In their list-like interface, all output is composed of brief transition clicks followed by short utterances describing the contents. These are truncated if a user performs additional input. Therefore, if a user interacts slowly, they hear the full description of the interface, while if they move rapidly then simply hear a sequence of clicks and aborted speech. Their approach appears to re-enable fluid, continuous, eyes-free interactions with the richness of speech output, something which has proven elusive in the past. Audio icon systems which present relatively long and informative snippets of sound, which are halted upon further user input have also been devised [1]. These examples suggest that rapid and low workload eyes-free interaction can only be achieved by experienced users of a system, and that incorporating a technique which enables novices to graduate to this status is an important aspect of eyes-free design.

3 Definition and Design Principles

This paper defines an eyes-free system as an interactive system with which experts can interact confidently in the absence of graphical feedback. The system should be aimed towards the general public, should feature an UI which enables a novice user to pick it up and use it immediately and should not rely on complex recognition technologies. We extend this definition with the following design principles:

1. Self monitored input: eyes-free input relies on the measurement of kinesthetic actions of the body: muscle tensions or the positions, orientations and movements of limbs. The bi-directional quality of the kinesthetic sense is what allows an expert user to monitor and mediate their input automatically and with confidence.

2. Input reflects bodily constraints: the control motions for an eyes-free interface should reflect the inherent characteristics of the motions of the body part being considered. The magnitude and stability of the motions, and the ease, and comfort with which they can be performed should be considered from the outset.

3. Minimal interaction models: eyes-free interaction models involve a simple, understandable mapping between a kinesthetic state and a system state. Metaphors (such as controlling the state of some virtual object like a cursor) should be kept to a minimum. The use of complex metaphors will detract from the correspondence between bodily and system states and will increase user reliance on the explicit cues generated by the system. This in turn will demand the deployment of more complex cues, which are likely to require additional cognitive resources to interpret.

4. Immediate output: eyes-free output is either immediate and short-lived or continually presented (and updated) as unobtrusive background information. Feedback needs to be displayed, and be capable of being absorbed, extremely rapidly. In cases where some external state immediately and noticeably changes as a result of the interaction, explicit feedback may not be necessary.

5. Seamless transition from novice to expert: fluid eyes-free interaction is the province of expert users of a system. It is important to provide a (possibly graphical) interface which enables novices to use the system straight away, but which also encourages them to seamlessly become experts who eventually no longer require it.

4 System Design: Eyes-Free Input with a Wearable Motion Sensor

Creating input devices for wearable computing systems is a challenging task. Input techniques need to be expressive, easy to learn and difficult to trigger accidentally, while input devices have to be small, lightweight and tough. High resolution graphical displays are unpractical in many scenarios while systems need to be expressive and easily understandable. Eyes-free interfaces are a natural fit with these criteria, and it is highly likely that future successful wearable interfaces will encompass eyes-free design elements. Reflecting this match, we explore the design of a wearable motion input system in light of the principles identified above.

Bodily motions that take place in free space can be captured by sensors such as accelerometers and gyroscopes and have considerable potential for wearable computing systems. The sensors are stand alone (unlike motion trackers or camera based systems) and are small, low power and low cost. It is relatively easy to embed them in articles of clothing or simple accessories such as watches or shoes so that they remain unobtrusive. Motion is also a rich six degree of freedom input channel theoretically capable of supporting a wide range of interactions.

Researchers have examined motion input for mobile devices using paradigms such as gesture recognition [7], text entry [22] and menu selection [9], [14]. Indeed, several mobile handsets, such as the Samsung SCH-S310, incorporating motion sensors have appeared. The literature is scarcer in the domain of wearable computing. In eyes-free themed work, Brewster et al. [1] studied simple head gestures coupled with an audio interface for the selection of different radio channels. Several authors have also presented solutions for wearable computing based around a wrist-mounted sensor pack. Rekimoto [15] describes an elegantly simple gesture recognition system reliant on static pose information captured from a motion sensor in conjunction with information about tensions in the wrist. Cheok et al. [2] describe a motion sensing platform in a number of different configurations, including one in which it is mounted on the wrist, but provide few specifics. Cho et al. [3] describe a wrist mounted gesture recognition system based on a simple conditional gesture recognition engine. Witt et al. [24] describe the preliminary design of a motion sensing system mounted on the back of the hand and report that users can comfortably perform simple conditional gestures to navigate around a graphically presented menu or control a cursor. The goal of their work is to develop a system to enable maintenance workers to access a computer without removing cumbersome protective apparel.

4.1 Overview

WristMenu is a prototype interaction technique based on input from a wrist mounted motion sensor, coupled with output on a vibrotactile display. It is based on a simple form of conditional gesture input and currently relies on a graphical display to allow users to seamlessly learn the interface. It is intended as a simple control interface for a wearable device, allowing users to issue commands and access a range of functionality rapidly and discretely. The technique is designed to be domain agnostic, and suitable for common wearable computing scenarios such as maintenance [24].

4.2 Designing Eyes-Free Input

The wrist is an appropriate body site for a wearable computing device; it is both easily accessible and socially acceptable. Wrist movement can include translations and rotations along and around all three spatial axes. However, compared to a device held in the hand, wrist-based motion input is impoverished; the hand itself is by far our most dexterous appendage. Furthermore, as the wrist is relatively distant from the elbow, the joint it rotates around, many of the motions it can make are relatively large in scale (although the just noticeable difference has been reported as low as 2 degrees [20]). For example, tilting a device held in the hand by 90 degrees is relatively simple in any axis, but subjecting a device mounted on the wrist to a similar experience will result in much more substantial, and potentially tiring and strenuous, motions.

Reflecting these concerns, our system focuses on one degree of freedom rotational motions made around the long axis of the forearm. These motions are relatively small scale, can be made quickly and have a comfortable range of around 90 degrees, from roughly palm down through until the palm is facing the body. Given the limited size and accuracy of the motions available, we split this area into 3 equally sized targets as shown in Figure 1. Each of these targets is situated in an easily distinguishable kinesthetic position: palm down, palm facing the body and in between these two states. Subsequently, the targets in these orientations are referred to as targets 1 (palm down), 2 (central) and 3 (palm facing body). This is shown in Figure 1.

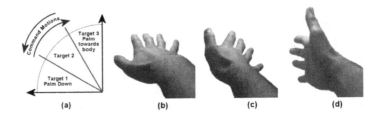

Fig 1. General control scheme for motions *(a)* and the three specific hand/forearm poses used in the system: selecting target 1 *(b)*, target 2 *(c)* and target 3 *(d)*.

Commands are composed of sequences of motions between the targets. Each command has three key points: the target it begins in, the target it ends in and optionally the target it turns in. This creates three classes of command, each of increasing complexity. In the first, the motion starts and ends in the same target without transitioning to another. In the second, it starts in a target, involves a motion to second target and then ends. In the third, it starts in one target, involves a motion to a second, a reversal of direction and an additional motion to a third target. These three classes can be seen in Figure 2. A total of 19 commands are available with this system.

4.3 Designing Eyes-Free Output

The system incorporates vibrotactile output to support eyes-free interaction. Two effects are implemented. The first is a simple, brief, click-like sensation on the transition between targets intended to provide awareness of state-changes in the system. The second is a continuous, unobtrusive, low amplitude vibration present on only the central target, allowing it to be unambiguously identified by users. Both attempt to convey the content of the commands to users, instead focusing on providing rapid feedback which will increase user confidence about the system state.

4.4 Designing Eyes-Free Command Structure

The system supports three classes of command, each requiring motions of increasing complexity to reach. It is clearly advantageous to place the most commonly accessed functionality under the simplest commands. The majority of commands are also nested beyond others: a total of 6 commands commence with the wrist held palm down, another 6 start with the palm facing the body and the remaining 7 from the central orientation. Organizing the commands to take advantage of this hierarchical structure is also likely to provide benefits to users; such relationships may aid the learning process. For example, if the system were used to control a personal music player, a common operation like toggling play/stop could be placed on target 1 (palm down). A closely related operation, such as skip to next track, could be activated by the command involving a movement from target 1 to target 2 (central target) and a less frequent operation, such as skip to previous track, could involve a movement from target 1 to target 2 and back again. This is shown in Figure 2.

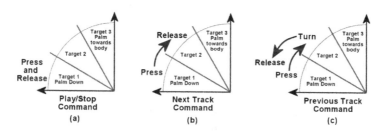

Fig. 2. Three WristMenu commands arranged in a hierarchy of motions and intended to control a portable music player. *(a)* shows a command which involves no motions, *(b)* a command which involves a motion to a second target and *(c)* a command with two motions separated by a turn.

4.5 Designing Graphical Learning Interface

As with marking menus, WristMenu relies on a graphical interface to enable users to learn its command set. This interface features a continually displayed three item menu bar, which shows the currently selected target and available commands. It is shown in Figure 3. As stroke origin is important, the basic concept relies on a continually displayed three item vertical icon bar. Highlighting indicates which icon is currently active. When a user engages the menu the display changes to show the currently available targets, one of which is already selected. Disengaging the menu immediately results in the activation of this highlighted command. The device can also be rotated until either of the other two commands is highlighted, and then disengaged to perform a selection. As the device is rotated, the icons in the menu change as different commands become available. A user can reverse their direction to select one these newly available commands. We believe this strategy of continually presenting commands options (together with careful design of the command structure) will allow novices to quickly grow used to the system and move towards expert user status.

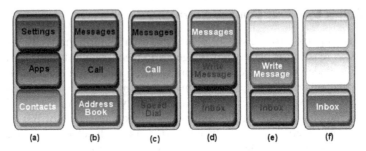

(a)   (b)   (c)   (d)   (e)   (f)

Fig. 3. Graphical interface to motion input system. In *(a)* the wrist is held palm down, the "Contacts" command group is selected and the system is not activated. In *(b)* the system is activated and available commands are shown. The user rotates through the central target *(c)* until the palm is facing the body *(d)*, then back through the central target *(e)* until the palm returns to its original position *(f)*. The "Inbox" command can then be activated. Light shading at the top of each command icon shows when the menu is activated, white text the currently active target and blank boxes motions beyond the scope of the system.

4.6   Prototype Implementation and Future Development

The WristMenu prototype was developed using an X-Sens MTi motion tracker [25], a matchbox sized sensor pack which includes three accelerometers that monitor lateral accelerations, including the constant 1G downwards due to gravity. By mounting this device on the wrist, and observing changes in the direction of gravity it is possible to infer the orientation of the wrist. WristMenu takes such measurements at 100Hz and uses a 5Hz low pass filter to eliminate sensor noise. A Tactaid VBW32 transducer [19] provides the vibrotactile cues. Both devices are currently attached to a desktop computer; the X-Sens provides its data through a USB connection and the Tactaid receives its signal from the audio out. The graphical interface is also presented on this computer, and commands are initiated and terminated by the press and release of a simple binary handheld switch. The sensor and transducer are shown in Figure 4.

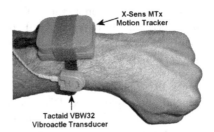

Fig 4. X-Sens MTx and Tactaid VWB32 used to produce WristMenu prototype

Immediate practical developments to this system will address these deficiencies. Porting to a wireless motion sensing platform such as that described Williamson *et al* [23] (which has an integrated vibrotactile display), or by Cho *et al.* [3] (with an integrated screen) will add true mobility. Given the extreme angles of motion used, flexible displays, which could curve around the wrist affording a clear view of the learning interface irrespective of wrist orientation, are also relevant. Formal evaluations are also an important next step. We are planning a series of evaluations on not only the basic feasibility of the system, but also its learnability, how effectively it can be used eyes free and how it compares with other input techniques. Given the constrained nature of the sensory and attentional resources they must consume, a multi-faceted approach to the evaluation of eyes-free interfaces is imperative.

5 Conclusions

This paper reviews the literature on eyes-free interaction, reflecting first on its origins and scope. It surveys the modalities previously used to build eyes-free systems and the general issues that affect them. It then tenders a working definition for this emerging domain, and a set of design principles. It concludes with a detailed case study of the design of an eyes-free interface for a wearable computing system based on motion input and tactile output.

The spread of computational power to new niches continues apace. As devices diversify, we believe that eyes-free interaction design will become increasingly important. It may become commonplace for certain classes of device to have no visual display, or certain classes of task be performed when our eyes are otherwise engaged. Specialist domains such as wearable computing could already benefit from better eyes-free design. By distilling the available literature into a more palatable form, this paper hopes to move this process forward and provide a set of criteria against which future researchers and system designers can position their work.

Acknowledgements

This work was supported by the IT R&D program of the Korean Ministry of Information and Communications (MIC) and Institute for Information Technology Advancement (IITA) (2005-S-065-03, Development of Wearable Personal Station).

References

1. Brewster, S., Lumsden, J., Bell, M., Hall, M., Tasker, S.: Multimodal 'eyes-free' interaction techniques for wearable devices. In: Proc. of CHI 2003, ACM Press, New York (2003)
2. Cheok, A.D., Ganesh Kumar, K., Prince, S.: Micro-Accelerometer Based Hardware Interfaces for Wearable Computer Mixed Reality Applications. In: Horrocks, I., Hendler, J. (eds.) ISWC 2002. LNCS, vol. 2342, Springer, Heidelberg (2002)
3. Cho, I., Sunwoo, J., Son, Y., Oh, M., Lee, C.: Development of a Single 3-axis Accelerometer Sensor Based Wearable Gesture Recognition Band. In: Proceedings of Ubiquitous Intelligence and Computing, Hong Kong (2007)
4. Crease, M.C., Brewster, S.A.: Making progress with sounds: The design and evaluation of an audio progress bar. In: Proc. of ICAD 1998, Glasgow, UK (1998)
5. Costanza, E., Inverso, S.A., Allen, R., Maes, P.: Intimate interfaces in action: assessing the usability and subtlety of emg-based motionless gestures. In: Proc. of CHI 2007, ACM Press, New York (2007)

6. Gaver, W.W., Smith, R.B, O'Shea, T.: Effective sounds in complex systems: the ARKOLA simulation. In: Proc. of CHI 1991, ACM Press, New York (1991)
7. Kallio, S., Kela, J., Mäntyjärvi, J., Plomp, J.: Visualization of hand gestures for pervasive computing environments. In: AVI 2006. Proceedings of the Working Conference on Advanced Visual interfaces, ACM Press, New York (2006)
8. Kurtenbach, G., Sellen, A., Buxton, W.: An empirical evaluation of some articulatory and cognitive aspects of "marking menus". Human Computer Interaction 8(1), 1–23 (1993)
9. Oakley, I., O'Modhrain, S.: Tilt to Scroll: Evaluating a Motion Based Vibrotactile Mobile Interface. In: Proceedings of World Haptics 2005, Pisa, Italy, IEEE Press, Los Alamitos (2005)
10. Oakley, I., Park, J.: The Effect of a Distracter Task on the Recognition of Tactile Icons. In: The proceedings of WorldHaptics 2007, Tsukuba, Japan, IEEE Press, IEEE Press (2007)
11. Oakley, I., Park, J.: A motion-based marking menu system. In: Extended Abstracts of CHI 2007, ACM Press, New York (2007)
12. Partridge, K., Chatterjee, S., Sazawal, V., Borriello, G., Want, R.: Tilt-Type: Accelerometer-Supported Text Entry for Very Small Devices. In: Proc. of ACM UIST, ACM Press, New York (2002)
13. Pirhonen, A., Brewster, S.A., Holguin, C.: Gestural and Audio Metaphors as a Means of Control for Mobile Devices. In: Proceedings of CHI 2002, ACM Press, New York (2002)
14. Poupyrev, I., Maruyama, S., Rekimoto, J.: Ambient touch: designing tactile interfaces for handheld devices. In: Proc. of ACM UIST 2002, ACM Press, New York (2002)
15. Rekimoto, J.: Gesturewrist and gesturepad: Unobtrusive wearable interaction devices. In: Proc. of ISWC 2001 (2001)
16. Roto, V., Oulasvirta, A.: Need for non-visual feedback with long response times in mobile HCI. In: proceedings of WWW 2005, ACM Press, New York (2005)
17. Smyth, T.N., Kirkpatrick, A.E.: A new approach to haptic augmentation of the GUI. In: Proceedings of ICMI 2006, ACM Press, New York (2006)
18. Sutcliffe, A.: On the effective use and reuse of HCI knowledge. ACM Trans. Comput.-Hum. Interact. 7(2), 197–221 (2000)
19. Tactaid VBW32, www.tactaid.com/skinstimulator.html
20. Tan, H.Z., Srinivasan, M.A., Eberman, B., Cheng, B.: Human factors for the design of force-reflecting haptic interfaces. In: Proceedings of ASME Dynamic Systems and Control Division, pp. 353–359. ASME, Chicago, IL (1994)
21. Watson, M., Sanderson, P.: Sonification Supports Eyes-Free Respiratory Monitoring and Task Time-Sharing. Human Factors 46(3), 497–517 (2004)
22. Wigdor, D., Balakrishnan, R.: TiltText: Using tilt for text input to mobile phones. In: Proc. of ACM UIST 2003, ACM Press, New York (2003)
23. Williamson, J., Murray-Smith, R., Hughes, S.: Shoogle: excitatory multimodal interaction on mobile devices. In: Proceedings CHI 2007., ACM Press, New York (2007)
24. Witt, H., Nicolai, T., Kenn, H.: Designing a Wearable User Interface for Hands-free Interaction in Maintenance Applications. In: Proceedings of IEEE International Conference on Pervasive Computing and Communications, IEEE Computer Society Press, Los Alamitos (2006)
25. Xsens Motion Technologies, www.xsens.com
26. Yin, M., Zhai, S.: The benefits of augmenting telephone voice menu navigation with visual browsing and search. In: Proc. of ACM CHI 2006, ACM Press, New York (2006)
27. Zhao, S., Dragicevic, P., Chignell, M., Balakrishnan, R., Baudisch, P.: Earpod: eyes-free menu selection using touch input and reactive audio feedback. In: Proceedings of CHI 2007, ACM Press, New York (2007)

Beyond Clicks and Beeps: In Pursuit of an Effective Sound Design Methodology

Antti Pirhonen[1], Kai Tuuri[1], Manne-Sakari Mustonen[1], and Emma Murphy[2]

[1] Department of Computer Science and Information Systems,
P.o. Box 35, FI-40014 University of Jyväskylä, Finland
{pianta,krtuuri,msmuston}@jyu.fi
[2] Sonic Arts Research Centre, Queen's University of Belfast, Belfast BT7 1NN,
Northern Ireland
e.murphy@qub.ac.uk

Abstract. Designing effective non-speech audio elements for a user-interface is a challenging task due to the complex nature of sounds and the changing contexts of non-visual interfaces. In this paper we present a design method, which is intended to take into account the complexity of audio design as well as the existing audio environment and the functional context of use. Central to this method is a rich use scenario, presented in the form of a radio play, which is used as a basis for the work of design panels. A previous version of the design method is analysed and specific practical issues are identified. Solutions to these issues are presented in the form of a modified version of the method. In the current version of the method, special attention has been paid to the development of a rich use scenario and the underlying personage. A case study is presented to illustrate the practical implementation of the modified design method and to support the proposed guidelines for its use.

1   Introduction

The inclusion of non-speech audio in user-interfaces (UIs) can be argued to have a fairly long tradition within the wider research field of human computer interaction. Despite its long history, the use of non-speech audio has not been established as an obvious part of UI conceptualisation in comparison to the use of graphic icons in visual design. There is an existing body of literature concerning the effective use of non-speech sounds in UI design, but most of this research details the design of warning signals or alarms only. The purpose of an auditory warning is to evoke attention only and therefore the amount of information to be conveyed is minimal. Detailed information about the cause for warning is usually provided in other forms. For instance, in a control room setting, an auditory warning is intended to direct attention to a visual display which gives information for the basis of possible action.

However, as intelligent devices decrease in size and go mobile, the roles of visuals and audio in UIs need to be revised. There is a clear need to develop knowledge on ways to present detailed information through the audio modality. Small devices cannot have large displays and in mobile settings, a user's gaze is often engaged in other duties and cannot continuously focus on a device. Furthermore, the development

I. Oakley and S. Brewster (Eds.): HAID 2007, LNCS 4813, pp. 133–144, 2007.

of applications for visually impaired users provides a strong motivation to convey detailed information through audio.

The central challenge of non-speech audio design is the lack of knowledge about the mapping between the physical properties and perceived qualities of sounds. It is difficult or impossible to extract independent dimensions of sound in order to construct auditory cues analytically. Although there are guidelines e.g. how to use rhythm and pitch to convey meanings for non-speech audio [1], these guidelines ignore all other dimensions of sounds. Information about the perception of individual properties of sound obviously contributes to design, but a more comprehensive view is also necessary to acquire effective designs.

Another practical need to have a comprehensive approach in the design of sounds is that the existing audio and functional environment needs to be taken into account in design. Sounds are usually designed with a view to being used to convey a message in a specific context. The same sound may work differently in altered contexts of use.

In our approach, a comprehensive view to the use context is accomplished in the form of a radio play. The approach is justified within a semiotic framework, within which the semantics of individual UI-sounds are pragmatically organised in relation to the functional and situational context. It has to be stressed that the use of the proposed method does not guarantee good design nor diminish the importance of sound design expertise. Rather, it provides new challenges for the designer, creating a new perspective to sound design.

In the first section of this paper, we outline the design method and its background. Then we illustrate the use of the method with the help of a design case. As the current version of the method is based on a previous one [2, 3], attention is paid to differences between the two versions. Finally, we draw conclusions about our experiences and present an agenda for further developments of the method.

2 Radio Play Method – The Background and Basic Principles

Use scenarios are considered a widely established means to understand the use of an application at a detailed level. The underlying objective involved in the preparation of use scenarios has traditionally been to cover as wide a variety of use cases as possible. These kinds of scenarios are based on the functional analysis of an application. They have proved to be effective in revealing aspects which would not have been noticed on the basis of purely technical specifications [4]. However, these kinds of descriptions are not of much use when considering specific parameters, e.g., the timbre of an individual UI-sound. More detailed, vivid use scenarios are needed to make it possible to identify with the user.

Alan Cooper's persona-approach [5] is an example of an approach that concentrates more on the user rather than the application. However, Cooper's idea is to cover as many user types as possible in creating a persona, which runs the risk of creating flat characters. Lene Nielsen tried to overcome these problems in her film manuscript approach [6]. The weakness in her approach – from the point of view of sound design – is that she was concentrating on overt behaviour of the user only, while in sound design attempting to capture the introspective dialogue and mental models of the user are essential.

In developing the ideas of Carroll, Cooper and Nielsen further to satisfy the needs of UI-sound design we have created a novel radio-play form, which incorporates use-scenario, persona and manuscript. Instead of a use-scenario we have defined the concept of a "rich use scenario". While traditional use scenarios aim at detecting use related issues, a rich use scenario is a means to get immersed in the life of the character and the use situation in particular. One major difference in this proposed approach is the number of use-scenarios created; while they traditionally are multiple, a rich use scenario is single. This is because a particular person and use case are the basis of design in the proposed method. These provide a common criterion for design decisions. In addition, since a radio play is an audio recording, it includes sounds other than narration. This property makes it possible to embed the sounds of an application into a radio play. Thus the concept of a radio play integrates all audio aspects of the use situation, into an immersive whole.

The proposed method involves the preparation of a manuscript (rich use scenario), three iterative design panel sessions, and the actual design of the sounds. In a previous version of this method, we have concentrated on the analysis of the panel sessions. The preparation of the manuscript alone – leaving aside any production of the radio play – played a minor role. However, in order to make the method more complete, in this paper we now focus on the preparation of the manuscript and related background work. As the final manuscript and radio-play influences many fundamental choices related to audio design (e.g. functions to be sonified and the purposes of sound in use situation), it is important to bring these *meta-design* issues into the scope of method.

3   Design Case: Sounds for Physical Browsing

Physical browsing (PB) is a concept, in which digital information is embedded at specific points in a physical environment [7]. The information is stored in passive radio frequency identification (RFID) tags, which can be read with a mobile device equipped with an RFID reader. In our case study, PB was applied to a museum environment. Our sound design study was to sonify the core functions of the PB application in a bicycle exhibition (called *Velomania*[1]) in a museum, which was constructed at a former engineering works.

The function of the PB application in the exhibition was to provide a visitor with additional information about certain objects. In practice, it meant that there would be RFID tags hidden behind visual icons referring to video or text. For instance, beside one bicycle there would be an icon which resembled a cine camera. Placing a device (PDA) close to the icon, the content of the tag was read into the device. The content was typically a URL, in which the actual content concerning the exhibition object was stored. After reading the URL, the content was downloaded to the device over a wireless local area network (WLAN).

The design process started with two visits to the museum, to familiarise ourselves with the environment and exhibition plans. During these visits, we recorded the audio environment, videoed and made notes. This was important in order to be able to begin to write a manuscript for the radio play. As there were no working

---

[1] http://www.tampere.fi/english/vapriikki/exhibitions/velomania.html

PB-implementations available for testing during this case study, the design team had to make assumptions based on available plans and specifications of the application.

At the very early stages of the case, we realised the need for a systematic structure in the form of a *checklist* to guide the creation of a use scenario. In the process of preparing the checklist the design team had fruitful discussions about many different issues related to the physical and cultural context of the exhibition. The functional concept of PB-application and its use in the exhibition, and of course the issue of a suitable character to be the *persona* of the scenario were among the key issues discussed. The outcome of that process was both the checklist-prototype itself (with accompanying theoretical justifications) and most importantly the team acquiring a mutual understanding of the use scenario. This was clearly the backlog of tasks required for the team to begin to create both the manuscript and the first level of audio design. A description of persona "Jari" was also made, and below is a short sample from it (translation from the original Finnish version):

> "...Before Jari moved to Tampere, he was active in a local culture association in Joensuu, which organised music concerts and relatively small independent culture events. After moving to Helsinki, he has not taken any active role in local culture associations, even though some of his friends have been asking him to join.
> Jari is an accustomed user of a mobile phone, and he has found mobile access to emails remarkably useful when he was organising events in Joensuu, because he had to keep in contact with several persons, mostly by email and telephone. Without mobile email, this would have been impossible. Even though he had found mobile emails and phones very useful, he dislikes computers due the difficult terminologies, which are confusing and frustrating. He does not find computers useful enough to justify the considerable learning effort involved. Despite this he has been actively involved in organising events; he prefers emails for communication rather than meetings, because he feels uncomfortable in crowds and face-to-face communication situations..."

In the case of Velomania the audio design task was quite straightforward. The central events to be sonified were discovered within the PB-concept and the actual technical specifications of PB-application. The events and descriptions of the preferred functionality of related sounds were listed and are presented below (see Table 1). A story was then written around the created persona and representative use situations of PB. Following the stage of adapting the story to the form of radio-play, it consisted mainly of spoken narration and background sound effects.

3.1 The Method for Creating the Rich Use Scenario

Here we present a short formal summary of the proposed method for creating a Rich Use Scenario and its adaptation to a radio-play. The fundamental idea in the design method is to achieve and explicate a common understanding within a design team about a use scenario. For that we propose the use of a specifically structured "checklist conversation". The purpose of this conversation is to launch the actual creative process and to prepare the required common ground for the design task. The nature of the conversation is an analytic and systematic roadmap of reminders and questions rather than a free brainstorming task for ideas. A checklist is used to remind or suggest relevant issues to be considered as part of the scope of the current scenario. A successful checklist conversation itself requires sufficient background knowledge about the context and current phase of concept design of the actual product.

Table 1. Sound design principles for the content reading task in PB

1. Event: successful reading of RFID-tag	
Functional type:	Feedback about user action
Functional semantics:	1a. reading of tag occurred ; 1b. physical pointing to the tag is no longer needed; 2. identification of tag type (video or html content)
Priorities:	Sound must have a clear attack that can be perceived accurately in synch with the actual event of reading. The duration of sound should be considered very short.
2. Process: download of the content	
Functional type:	Sonificated process
Functional semantics:	1a. device is doing something; 1b. "wait, almost ready"; 2. the stage of downloading process (if technically possible)
Priorities.	Sound starts and stops along with downloading. The start of the process requires user action (a push of a button). Therefore sound has more orientating function and evoking attention is not necessary.
3. Event: download ready	
Functional type:	Notice
Functional semantics:	1. download is ready; 2. draw attention back to device
Priorities:	Because attention of the user is likely to be close to the device already due to required user action for downloading, it's not necessary to use too much attention grabbing. The synchronisation of sound and event of finishing is meaningful but not critical. Clear point of attack was needed in event 1 but it is not necessity here. Similarly the criteria for a short sound duration is not so strict. The sound may be needed to be "open".

The checklist was divided into three equally weighted parts:

1. Context: the physical and cultural environment where the scenario takes place (including the soundscape)
2. Functional concept: functionalities of the current application/ product from the viewpoint of use situation and the possible role of sound in the user interface
3. Persona: considerations of abilities, background, status, personality, values, likes/ dislikes and other dispositions of the persona and their likely effects in relation to the use scenario

Based on this list, we prepared a detailed *checklist conversation* which launches off the creative process. This can be conceptualised as three distinct threads: 1) analysis of context 2) meta-design of functions of sounds (derived from functional concept) and 3) creation of a persona for the story (Rich Use Scenario). The creation of the persona should be started as an intuitively made short stub-description, which can be enriched along with the writing of the story. The purpose of the third thread is to be the backbone of story creation and essentially to wrap the other two threads into the story using the process of convergence in creative writing. The outcome of the checklist conversation does not necessary need to be formally presented or fully documented. After the conversation, the main purpose of the checklist is to work as a cognitive map that refers to discussed issues.

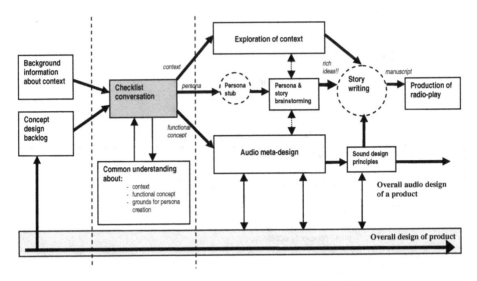

Fig. 1. The process of creating Rich Use Scenario

The thread of sound meta-design should be seen as a starting point of the overall audio design of a product. During the creation of the use scenario the definitions of "events-to-be-sonified" and the functional purposes of sounds in the given context should be listed. As a part of the proposed method we suggest preparation of a formal document about sound design principles in which all context- and concept-derived fundamentals and priorities for sound design are clearly explicated. This is also critically required information for writing the contextual orientation around the soundpoints in the story. To prevent audio from becoming a minor added-on feature, the checklist conversation should take place when decisions of the use of sensory modalities in UI (visual, auditory, haptic) are still open.

When the story is finished it should be formulated as a radio play manuscript. In the current case, the manuscript consisted of the written story and soundpoints for effects to-be-designed. To achieve more interesting results, it is recommended to consider sound effects at the initial stage of written manuscript as a means to recreate the sonic backgrounds as well as mental imagery for narration. Mere use of spoken narration can be tiresome so it should not be used extensively. The expressive quality of narration also matters therefore a voice-actor is preferred. And of course, for use at panel work, predefined soundpoints of UI-sounds are supposed to remain "empty" in the radio-play.

3.2 Panel Work

An essential part of the proposed method is a series of panel sessions. In the previous version of the method [2, 3], this implied three iterative sessions with different panellists each time. The rich use scenario, or radio play, had a different kind of role in each session. In this original version of the method, the UI-sounds were part of the radio-play, but at the first panel session there were none available. The story was heard to have only a brief pause at the points where the sounds to be designed were supposed to take place. The task of the panel was to bring out ideas of what these sounds should be like. The second panel used the same story, but this time draft sounds, designed on the basis of the ideas of the first panel, were presented as part of the radio play. After the second panel, the draft sounds were further developed and the resulting, more finalised sounds were presented to the third panel, whose role was to react and evaluate these sounds.

Although the panel work in the previous design case contributed to the actual sound design, we found several problems in the method which needed to be solved.

1. The most practical problem was the organisation of the panel session; listening to the radio-play and adding sounds was technically complicated for the moderators running the sessions.
2. The orientation of the panellists. Before a panel session, panellists were told that their task was to design or give ideas of sound effects for a radio play. There was no description about the application, because we wanted the panellists to concentrate on the story, not to think about an application. In this way, we wished to get more divergent ideas than by figuring out an application i.e., we were trying to forget stereotypical, clumsy beeps which we are used to in many familiar gadgets. However, many of our panellists were computer scientists and the sessions were organised in either a department of computing or in an interdisciplinary, but technically oriented research centre. As a result, some of the discussions in the panel sessions were orientated around the application design, without reference to the presented story. Therefore we concluded that more effort should be spent on making the panellists immerse themselves in the radio play.
3. Using different panellists in each session was intended to result in more ideas and validating those ideas within a larger group. However, it turned out that when the first panel presented an idea which was implemented for the second or third panel, the later ones did not necessarily understand the original idea. If the panellists were the same in each session, they could have developed their own ideas further. Also, using the same panellists could have enabled the panellists to see the concrete result of their own work, thus leading to higher motivation.

In the current study, we responded to the observed problems of the previous version of the method (listed above, reported in detail in [3]) in the following ways:

1. We developed the *ScenarioPlayer* application for the management and control of radio play. The aim was to create a tool, with the help of which the moderator of the panel sessions could effortlessly play the radio play, seek a play position and choose among a selection of sound effects. In this way, the moderator was supposed to be able to concentrate on the interaction among panellists instead of on technical issues.
2. The invitation to participate in the panels was distributed to student email lists within different faculties and departments in the University of Jyväskylä. Invited departments included music, teacher education, history, communication, information systems and psychology. To prevent the panellists from associating the panels with computing, we organised the sessions in the department of music. Also, we paid attention to the wording of the invitation e-mail.

3. Certainly using different panellists in each session has benefits to the design method, but on this occasion we wanted to try using same panellists for every session.

Each participant was promised to be rewarded with 2 movie tickets for three, approximately one hour sessions. Despite the minor compensation, 6 students signed up. They represented communication studies (3 students), psychology, and political science. 5 of these were female. The only male participant was the student of political science.

Table 2. The progress of panel sessions

Session 1:	Session 2:	Session 3:
Introducing of the panellists - Only two panellists knew each other in advance Warming-up - Listening of three different soundscape, after which the panellists were asked to describe what they "saw" Listening of radio play - First once through, then another time by pausing in blank soundpoints, discussing what the sound could be like Instructions for homework - Participants were asked to stop to listen some soundscape or individual sound in their everyday environment, and prepare themselves to tell about the experience in the next session.	Warming up - Checking the homework: Each participant told about certain sound or soundscape Listening of radio play with first draft sounds - Each soundpoint was listened several times, with different alternative sounds. - Pros and cons of each alternative were listed on a flap board.	Evaluation of radio play with the elaborated sounds - Pros and cons listed on a flap board Evaluation of combinations of sounds - Two alternative combinations of three closely related sound points were discussed as groups of sounds rather than as individual sounds Questionnaire concerning the panel sessions - Explicit feedback for the needs of developing the method

The panel work was scheduled within one week: one hour sessions on Monday, Wednesday and Friday mornings. The timing was a compromise between two conflicting objectives: to enable the discussion to continue from session to session there should not be a long break between the sessions On the other hand, the design team needed to design sounds between the panels, and one whole working day was the shortest acceptable time for that.

There were many differences in the organisation of the panel sessions while using the same panellists all the time (compared to using different panellists as we did in the previous case study [3]). The timetable consideration, mentioned above was one; another major difference was the actual agenda for each session. In our previous case study, we started each session so that the participants did not have more information about the task than a brief invitation. Now only the first session was like that. In the following sessions, the participants had developed strong expectations from the first panel. Another crucial difference was the fact that the story of the radio play was already familiar, as well as other participants and the nature of work involved in the panel sessions.

As we had more time with each panellist, three hours altogether, we could afford to spend some time at the beginning of the first and second panel with short warming-up tasks. The objectives of these tasks were to sensitise hearing and to train participants to verbally describe non-speech sounds.

3.3 Initial Findings of the Panel Sessions

The findings presented here are based on early reflections of empirical panel experiences. Panel sessions were recorded for purposes of further analysis of group communication, group dynamics and panel discussions.

From observations we found that group discussion is a suitable method for dealing with subjective connotations and meanings of sound. Although there is a risk that group situations can actually lead to diminished creativity [8], we found that the group offered support for participators to communicate their thoughts and refine presented ideas by cooperative comments. Generating ideas and thoughts about sounds appeared most fluent when sounds were actually presented to the panellists. Discussion among panellists was then mostly concerned with the associations and connotations regarding the sounds presented to them. Considering this, the panel discussion method is easiest to be used in an evaluation, or evaluation based design, rather than designing sound ideas from the scratch.

An interesting observation was that panellists evaluated sounds by different criteria; on the basis of freely evoked connotations and mental images or possible sound sources, or whether the sound was aesthetically pleasant/ not pleasant, or sounds were evaluated whether they were suitable for the functional context or combination of other sounds. Preferred sounds varied noticeably when considered with different criteria. These observations further confirmed the importance of the whole context of use in UI sound design. On the other hand, emphasising the context or application in the panel sessions too strongly, may stifle creative ideas. If the panellists evaluate the sounds only by the criteria of what is clearly suitable for the context, the group may reject certain ideas when they do not fit into context perfectly from the beginning.

Panellists were motivated by the tasks maybe because they could notice that their opinion was taken into account during the sound production between the panels. The "ear opening" warming-up tasks of the first panel session and homework task for the second session were utilised as *motivational orientation* [9] for the panellists to get immersed in the sound design process and to consider sounds more effectively through the panel sessions. The panellists also found that the sounds became more interesting as they developed. Warming-up tasks had an additional important function; they contributed to group cohesion and broke the ice for the group to concentrate on actual panel tasks. Still, communication remained very moderator-dependent and group-centric. If more self-organised group work could be achieved, it might lead to more fluent and moderator-independent discussion. However, it should be noticed that structured sessions usually produce more creative results than unstructured ones as shown in studies of creative group work [8]. So, the structure is needed but what is the right kind of structure for creative panel work?

Group dynamics play a considerably important role in this design method. The composition of group, the structure of panel session and the role of moderator are key elements in the sense of methodological development. Problems may arise e.g. when panellists feel themselves too distant from each other, or when they seek too much group harmony (the effect of *groupthink*), or when ideas are not communicated due to a critical climate [10]. Furthermore the moderator has a demanding role in not leading the panellists towards a particular direction, but still encouraging panellists to discuss openly and equally. However, when the orientation of group work is evaluative, the moderator should provide indirect support for dissents to enable and manage *creative conflicts* [8]. Widely used group discussion method of focus groups [11] have many methodological similarities to the panel sessions presented in this study. This literature could offer tried and tested frameworks for future development of the current method.

If the sound designer provides only the sounds s/he favours, there is a risk it may appear to the panellists as preferred direction. It should be taken into consideration, that sounds to be presented in a panel session must consist of sufficiently divergent material. In the current case, a very tight time-table of panel sessions made the design and implementation of several different draft-sounds (based on the ideas from previous panel session) quite rushed.

4   Discussion and Concluding Statements

In this paper a previously proposed [3] method for designing UI-sounds has been revised in many ways. In the previous version of the method, the preparation of a Rich Use Scenario relied purely on the design team's existing skills in writing an inspiring story. Having now continued with the development of the method, we are able to provide some clear guidelines for the writing process.

For any successful audio design it is essential to work closely with the overall design concepts from a sufficiently early stage. Audio-orientated designer(s) should be involved in the concept design to benefit the full potential of audio in the implementation of a UI. The proposed method provides a comprehensive way of incorporating audio design to the whole UI development process. However the same approach could be applied to the design of other non-visual UI-elements, such as tactile cues. For example a slightly modified method has proved to be promising in the design of haptic feedback [12].

As in the previous version of the method, design panels are not created to replace the work of a professional sound designer. Panel sessions are tools for a sound designer to use them either for creative inspiration or evaluation or both. Ultimately, it is up to sound designer to judge the best way to utilise the output of panels in each case. The creative continuum of sound design starts with divergent situation with wealth of different design possibilities and unfound ideas. As the process goes on, divergence diminishes gradually when the pressure to get convergent solutions rises. Panel sessions can be placed along that continuum according to what is their main role; design or evaluation (see Figure 2).

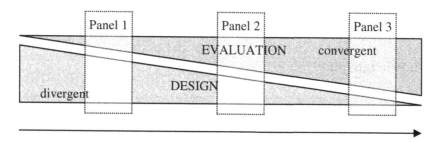

Fig. 2. Design-evaluation continuum

The position of a certain panel in the design-evaluation continuum and gaps of time between panels are notable factors in defining goals for each panel session. Panels can be used in the way that the method originally proposed [3]; for triggering ideas and then evaluate and refine them in two additional iterations. Alternatively, this setting can be modified to two different directions: Firstly, more weight can be put into idea generation e.g. by allocating (at least) two panel sessions for idea generation. The first session should be used to familiarise the panel with the problem to be solved, and the second session to brainstorm for developed ideas and insights. The second option should give sufficient time for individual idea-incubation of panellists before the actual group brainstorming. It is also recommended [9] to separate idea generation clearly from evaluation to prevent a critical and narrow communication climate. Or secondly, panels can be used for purely evaluation purposes by providing a set of sounds or ideas for the basis of discussion. Our empirical findings indicate that evaluative orientation also facilitates the verbal expression about sound-related ideas. i.e., evaluating existing sounds does not exclude the possibility for gaining new ideas.

The role assigned to user panels is highly dependent on the nature of the design case. In some cases, there are strict limitations concerning the different qualities of sound. For instance, it can be a standard (like in the alarms of safety critical systems) or technical limitation (like the sound generation capacity of wrist computers). Then the number of different kinds of alternative sounds may be limited and the work of the panels could be based on the evaluation of the available alternatives. Otherwise, when designing completely novel consumer product concepts, the best policy is to start the panel work with as open a mind as possible. The nature of the design case presented in this paper is closer to the later description.

In the design case presented in this paper we found it a good idea to use the same panellists in all panel sessions. The main advantages of using the same people is that the panellists have more time to immerse themselves in the design case and to learn to listen to their audio environment. This became clear from the formal feedback we collected from the panellists. Furthermore the idea of using the same panellists enhances the original aims of the method to trigger creativity rather than achieving generic agreement from users. However, if the task of the panels is based on the evaluation of readily designed sounds, large number of panellists, i.e., different panellists in each session, would probably be worth considering. To confirm that assumption, more design cases will need to be carried out. We are therefore currently planning cases, in which the panels might be given a more evaluative role.

Acknowledgments

We are more than grateful to the wonderful panellists, who really threw themselves to the panel work.

This work is funded by Finnish Funding Agency for Technology and Innovation (www.tekes.fi), Eduserv (www.eduserv.org.uk), and the following partners: Nokia Ltd., GE Healthcare Finland Ltd., Sunit Ltd., Suunto Ltd., and Tampere city council.

References

1. Brewster, S., Wright, P., Edwards, A.: Experimentally derived guidelines for the creation of earcons. In: Adjunct Proceedings of HCI 1995, Huddersfield, UK, pp. 155–159 (1995)
2. Pirhonen, A., Murphy, E., McAllister, G., Yu, W.: Non-speech sounds as elements of a use scenario: a semiotic perspective. In: Proceedings of ICAD 2006, London, June 20-23 2006, pp. 20–23 (2006) (CD-rom format)
3. Murphy, E., Pirhonen, A., McAllister, G., Yu, W.A: semiotic approach to the design of non-speech sounds. In: McGookin, D., Brewster, S. (eds.) HAID 2006. LNCS, vol. 4129, pp. 121–132. Springer, Heidelberg (2006)
4. Carroll, J.M.: Making use: Scenario based design of human-computer interactions. MIT Press, Cambridge (2000)
5. Cooper, A.: The inmates are running the asylum: Why high-tech products drive us crazy and how to restore the sanity. Sams, Indianapolis, IN (2004)
6. Nielsen, L.: From user to character: an investigation into user-descriptions in scenarios. In: Proceedings of the conference on Designing interactive systems: processes, practices, methods, and techniques, London, 25-28.6.2002, pp. 99–104. ACM Press, New York (2002)
7. Välkkynen, P.: Hovering: Visualising RFID hyperlinks in a mobile phone. In: Rukzio, E., Paolucci, M., Finin, T., Wisner, P., Payne, T. (eds.) Proceedings of MIRW 2006, Espoo, Finland, September 12, 2005, pp. 27–29 (2005)
8. Levi, D.: Group Dynamics for Teams. Sage Publications, Thousand Oaks, CA (2001)
9. Amabile, T.: Creativity in context. Westview, Boulder, CO (1996)
10. Forsyth, D.: Group Dynamics. 3rd edn. Wadsworth, Belmont, CA (1999)
11. Fern, E.: Advanced Focus Group Research. Sage Publications Inc., Thousand Oaks, CA (2001)
12. Kuber, R., Yu, W., McAllister, G.: Towards developing assistive haptic feedback for visually impaired internet users. In: CHI 2007. Proceedings of the SIGCHI Conference on Human Factors in Computing Systems, San Jose, California, USA, April 28 - May 03, 2007, pp. 1525–1534. ACM Press, New York (2007)

Author Index

Lecture Notes in Computer Science

Sublibrary 3: Information Systems and Application, incl. Internet/Web and HCI

For information about Vols. 1– 4365
please contact your bookseller or Springer

Vol. 4602: S. Barker, G.-J. Ahn (Eds.), Data and Applications Security XXI. X, 291 pages. 2007.

Vol. 4601: S. Spaccapietra, P. Atzeni, F. Fages, M.-S. Hacid, M. Kifer, J. Mylopoulos, B. Pernici, P. Shvaiko, J. Trujillo, I. Zaihrayeu (Eds.), Journal on Data Semantics IX. XV, 197 pages. 2007.

Vol. 4592: Z. Kedad, N. Lammari, E. Métais, F. Meziane, Y. Rezgui (Eds.), Natural Language Processing and Information Systems. XIV, 442 pages. 2007.

Vol. 4587: R. Cooper, J. Kennedy (Eds.), Data Management. XIII, 259 pages. 2007.

Vol. 4577: N. Sebe, Y. Liu, Y.-t. Zhuang, T.S. Huang (Eds.), Multimedia Content Analysis and Mining. XIII, 513 pages. 2007.

Vol. 4568: T. Ishida, S. R. Fussell, P. T. J. M. Vossen (Eds.), Intercultural Collaboration. XIII, 395 pages. 2007.

Vol. 4566: M.J. Dainoff (Ed.), Ergonomics and Health Aspects of Work with Computers. XVIII, 390 pages. 2007.

Vol. 4564: D. Schuler (Ed.), Online Communities and Social Computing. XVII, 520 pages. 2007.

Vol. 4563: R. Shumaker (Ed.), Virtual Reality. XXII, 762 pages. 2007.

Vol. 4561: V.G. Duffy (Ed.), Digital Human Modeling. XXIII, 1068 pages. 2007.

Vol. 4560: N. Aykin (Ed.), Usability and Internationalization, Part II. XVIII, 576 pages. 2007.

Vol. 4559: N. Aykin (Ed.), Usability and Internationalization, Part I. XVIII, 661 pages. 2007.

Vol. 4558: M.J. Smith, G. Salvendy (Eds.), Human Interface and the Management of Information, Part II. XXIII, 1162 pages. 2007.

Vol. 4557: M.J. Smith, G. Salvendy (Eds.), Human Interface and the Management of Information, Part I. XXII, 1030 pages. 2007.

Vol. 4541: T. Okadome, T. Yamazaki, M. Makhtari (Eds.), Pervasive Computing for Quality of Life Enhancement. IX, 248 pages. 2007.

Vol. 4537: K.C.-C. Chang, W. Wang, L. Chen, C.A. Ellis, C.-H. Hsu, A.C. Tsoi, H. Wang (Eds.), Advances in Web and Network Technologies, and Information Management. XXIII, 707 pages. 2007.

Vol. 4531: J. Indulska, K. Raymond (Eds.), Distributed Applications and Interoperable Systems. XI, 337 pages. 2007.

Vol. 4526: M. Malek, M. Reitenspieß, A. van Moorsel (Eds.), Service Availability. X, 155 pages. 2007.

Vol. 4524: M. Marchiori, J.Z. Pan, C.d.S. Marie (Eds.), Web Reasoning and Rule Systems. XI, 382 pages. 2007.

Vol. 4519: E. Franconi, M. Kifer, W. May (Eds.), The Semantic Web: Research and Applications. XVIII, 830 pages. 2007.

Vol. 4518: N. Fuhr, M. Lalmas, A. Trotman (Eds.), Comparative Evaluation of XML Information Retrieval Systems. XII, 554 pages. 2007.

Vol. 4508: M.-Y. Kao, X.-Y. Li (Eds.), Algorithmic Aspects in Information and Management. VIII, 428 pages. 2007.

Vol. 4506: D. Zeng, I. Gotham, K. Komatsu, C. Lynch, M. Thurmond, D. Madigan, B. Lober, J. Kvach, H. Chen (Eds.), Intelligence and Security Informatics: Biosurveillance. XI, 234 pages. 2007.

Vol. 4505: G. Dong, X. Lin, W. Wang, Y. Yang, J.X. Yu (Eds.), Advances in Data and Web Management. XXII, 896 pages. 2007.

Vol. 4504: J. Huang, R. Kowalczyk, Z. Maamar, D. Martin, I. Müller, S. Stoutenburg, K.P. Sycara (Eds.), Service-Oriented Computing: Agents, Semantics, and Engineering. X, 175 pages. 2007.

Vol. 4500: N.A. Streitz, A.D. Kameas, I. Mavrommati (Eds.), The Disappearing Computer. XVIII, 304 pages. 2007.

Vol. 4495: J. Krogstie, A. Opdahl, G. Sindre (Eds.), Advanced Information Systems Engineering. XVI, 606 pages. 2007.

Vol. 4480: A. LaMarca, M. Langheinrich, K.N. Truong (Eds.), Pervasive Computing. XIII, 369 pages. 2007.

Vol. 4473: D. Draheim, G. Weber (Eds.), Trends in Enterprise Application Architecture. X, 355 pages. 2007.

Vol. 4471: P. Cesar, K. Chorianopoulos, J.F. Jensen (Eds.), Interactive TV: A Shared Experience. XIII, 236 pages. 2007.

Vol. 4469: K.-c. Hui, Z. Pan, R.C.-k. Chung, C.C.L. Wang, X. Jin, S. Göbel, E.C.-L. Li (Eds.), Technologies for E-Learning and Digital Entertainment. XVIII, 974 pages. 2007.

Vol. 4443: R. Kotagiri, P. Radha Krishna, M. Mohania, E. Nantajeewarawat (Eds.), Advances in Databases: Concepts, Systems and Applications. XXI, 1126 pages. 2007.

Vol. 4439: W. Abramowicz (Ed.), Business Information Systems. XV, 654 pages. 2007.

Vol. 4430: C.C. Yang, D. Zeng, M. Chau, K. Chang, Q. Yang, X. Cheng, J. Wang, F.-Y. Wang, H. Chen (Eds.), Intelligence and Security Informatics. XII, 330 pages. 2007.

Vol. 4425: G. Amati, C. Carpineto, G. Romano (Eds.), Advances in Information Retrieval. XIX, 759 pages. 2007.

Vol. 4412: F. Stajano, H.J. Kim, J.-S. Chae, S.-D. Kim (Eds.), Ubiquitous Convergence Technology. XI, 302 pages. 2007.

Vol. 4402: W. Shen, J.-Z. Luo, Z. Lin, J.-P.A. Barthès, Q. Hao (Eds.), Computer Supported Cooperative Work in Design III. XV, 763 pages. 2007.

Vol. 4398: S. Marchand-Maillet, E. Bruno, A. Nürnberger, M. Detyniecki (Eds.), Adaptive Multimedia Retrieval: User, Context, and Feedback. XI, 269 pages. 2007.

Vol. 4397: C. Stephanidis, M. Pieper (Eds.), Universal Access in Ambient Intelligence Environments. XV, 467 pages. 2007.

Vol. 4380: S. Spaccapietra, P. Atzeni, F. Fages, M.-S. Hacid, M. Kifer, J. Mylopoulos, B. Pernici, P. Shvaiko, J. Trujillo, I. Zaihrayeu (Eds.), Journal on Data Semantics VIII. XV, 219 pages. 2007.